1000 Fact
Stranger Things

Nick Bryce

Contents

PREFACE

Stranger Things is science fiction horror show that streams on Netflix. It is a love letter to 80s pop culture - most specifically Stephen King, Steven Spielberg, and John Carpenter. Its range of influences is vast though and takes in everything from John Hughes to Lovecraft to Clive Barker to Project MKUltra. 1000 Facts About Stranger Things contains one thousand fascinating and eclectic facts that encompass all facets of this amazingly popular show. If you think you know absolutely everything there is to know about Stranger Things then this book would beg to differ! Hopefully there will be plenty here that is new - even to the most dedicated Stranger Things superfan.

The facts that follow are diverse and cover all aspects of the show. Cast, crew, music, Easter eggs, stunts, behind the scenes, observations, fan theories, characters, casting, Dungeons & Dragons, games, merch, goofs, viewing figures, episodes, seasons, production notes, origins, and so on. The premise of Stranger Things is relatively simple on the surface - despite the scientific trappings and numerous pop culture Easter eggs.

Dredging up inspiration from many novels, stories, movies, tv shows, and video games, the show concerns a group of characters in a small (and fictional) Indiana town named Hawkins. The local Department of Energy - in the form of the Hawkins Lab - has opened a dimensional rift (rather like in Stephen King's The Mist) which is a portal to a hostile and nightmare version of our own world. A faceless monster (which the boys in the show dub the Demogorgon because of their love of Dungeons & Dragons) begins to move to and thro from this world and ours.

A little boy named Will Byers is pulled into the other dimension (dubbed the Upside Down by the kids) and so a search for him begins with police chief Hopper, his mother

Joyce Byers, and Will's friends all conducting their own investigations. Into this mix we throw Eleven, a little girl with telekinetic powers who escaped from the Hawkins Lab. She is secretly sheltered by Will's friends and might be the key to finding him. A teenager named Barb is also snared by the monster and her friend Nancy also becomes embroiled in seeking to get to the bottom of the strange events happening around the fringes of this small town.

Season two is a slightly more expansive affair and concerns the 'Mind Flayer' (aka the Shadow Monster) - a huge terrifying 'big boss' of the Upside Down who possesses Will. Once again, Hawkins is infiltrated by Upside Down creatures and all hell breaks loose. Season three throws a neon drenched shopping mall and Cold War baddies from the Soviet Union into the mix and as for season four, well, Stranger Things 4 is the biggest and boldest season yet. The book that follows contains a positive slew of facts about all four seasons of Stranger Things.

Despite the many influences of Stranger Things (which the show doesn't shy away from), it still feels unique enough to stand on its own feet. There is genuine horror, action, and plenty of wit from both the cast and the scripts. The show is beautifully designed and has a memorable synth score by Survive. At its best, Stranger Things is about as much fun as a tv show can get and each new season is eagerly anticipated (and rapidly binged when it arrives). So, let's go ahead and wallow in Stranger Things and the wonderful world it has created. Hopefully there will be plenty of facts and trivia in this book that even the most dedicated of fans might not have known before.

1000 FACTS ABOUT STRANGER THINGS

(1)

Dustin Henderson's trucker cap in the first two seasons was kept secure in a special box between Gaten Matarazzo's scenes because the costume department were rather paranoid about losing it. They evidently didn't have an exact duplicate.

(2)

It is estimated that Millie Bobby Brown only had dialogue for about three minutes of Eleven's total screentime in season one. Eleven has more screentime (about sixty minutes) than anyone in season one so this is pretty remarkable.

(3)

Gaten Matarazzo said that on Stranger Things they are supplied with authentic vintage 1980s underwear by the costume department but he deduced at some point he was the only cast member who was actually bothering to wear it.

(4)

Stranger Things makeup artist Amy L. Forsythe said she came up with her own backstory concerning who did Eleven's makeup for the Snow Ball dance in Stranger Things 2. Amy said that Hopper would obviously have no clue about makeup and so probably asked Nancy. Nancy, in turn, probably borrowed some makeup from her mother Karen.

This then, in a circuitous way, provides a perfectly logical explanation for why Eleven has purple eyeshadow at the Snow Ball!

(5)

The term "Demogorgon" first appeared in the 4th Century Latin poem Thebaid by Placidus. The poem described a demon who must not be named (which is all very Lovecraftian).

(6)

In season three, Dacre Montgomery as Billy Hargrove has a skull tattoo on his arm. Originally, the skull was going to have an eyepatch. In the end though they decided to veto the eyepatch because they felt it might come across as too much of an on the nose reference to The Goonies.

(7)

Amy L. Forsythe said that the fertilizer we see Mrs Driscoll eating in Stranger Things 3 was in reality made up of pulse honey almond granola, chocolate powder, espresso coffee grounds, and various food dyes. It was difficult to concoct this mixture because it obviously had to be edible for the actress but also still look like real fertilizer.

(8)

Shannon Purser as Barb Holland only had about thirty lines of dialogue in her time on the show.

(9)

The mouth and the head of the Demogorgon in Stranger Things somewhat resembles a Rafflesia arnoldi. Rafflesia arnoldii, the corpse flower or giant padma, is a species of flowering plant in the parasitic genus Rafflesia.

(10)

The makeup department on Stranger Things have varying viscosities of fake blood for Eleven's nosebleeds. This is so they can control how fast and how far the blood drips.

(11)

The Demogorgon in Dungeons & Dragons has two heads. The heads are named Aemeul and Hethradiah.

(12)

Gaten Matarazzo said that Dustin Henderson only had two lines in the first script he read for Stranger Things (or Montauk as it would have been called at the time). The character of Dustin was obviously expanded into a much bigger part. Gaten said his agent was very annoyed when he was cast as Dustin rather than Mike or Lucas in Stranger Things because the agent presumed the part of Dustin was quite a minor part. It all turned out fine in the end

(13)

When they wanted to give Will Byers a green tongue in Stranger Things 2 to convey the dark possessed version of the character, the makeup department experimented with sucking rainbow-coloured lollipops to see if this would have the desired effect. However the lollipops didn't turn out to be consistent enough in their effect so in the end they used green cake frosting to give Noah Schnapp a murky looking tongue.

(14)

The Demogorgon killing Barb while Nancy is upstairs with Steve in season one is a twist on the vintage horror movie trope where the most promiscuous characters are usually bumped off first.

(15)

The retro Reebok sneakers Millie Bobby Brown wears as Eleven in Stranger Things 3 were exceptionally hard to find and eventually purchased by the costume department at a vintage Atlanta market. Atlanta is where Stranger Things, despite being set in Indiana, is shot.

(16)

Over fifty million people around the world have played the board game Dungeons & Dragons since it was invented in 1974.

(17)

In 2014 it was estimated that the Eggo brand had a 60% share of the frozen waffle market in the United States. This market share would soon increase even further in the years to come thanks to Stranger Things. By then the Eggo brand had long since been sold to Kelloggs.

(18)

Finn Wolfhard said he somehow managed to cut his chin on a desk around the time they made season one of Stranger Things so this had to be covered up by makeup.

(19)

The Hawkins school science teacher's name (Scott Clarke) is a mash-up of the film director Ridley Scott and science fiction author Arthur C. Clarke.

(20)

In the seventies there was a secret program called Project Stargate which attempted to see if mind readers and psychics could be used to spy on the Soviet Union. The famous 'spoon bender', illusionist and alleged psychic Uri Geller was a part of these experiments. The Duffer Brothers patently read about all of these types of secret projects and incorporated them into the mythology of Stranger Things.

(21)

Millie Bobby Brown said that when she finished shooting the first season of Stranger Things she went back to England and genuinely wondered if she would ever get another acting job again. She had no idea that Stranger Things was going to become such a sensation and make her so famous.

(22)

The walkie-talkies that the boys use in season of Stranger Things were purchased at a Long Beach flea market by the prop master Lynda Reiss.

(23)

Eleven was initially only supposed to steal one box of Eggos from the store in season one but Millie Bobby Brown thought the scene would work better if Eleven picked up more boxes.

(24)

Gaten Matarazzo said that when they were shooting season one of Stranger Things there were a few comical mishaps with the long antenna on the walkie-talkies. He said Millie Bobby Brown in particular got clobbered a few times by accident.

(25)

The character of Eleven is estimated to have killed around twenty people in the first three seasons of Stranger Things.

(26)

The first sensory deprivation tank (or chamber) was invented by John C. Lilly in 1954. Lily was an American physician, neuroscientist, psychoanalyst, psychonaut, philosopher, writer and inventor. The idea of sensory deprivation tanks is that you are removed from all external stimuli as a means to explore the nature of human consciousness.

Sensory deprivation tanks obviously play a big part in the first season of Stranger Things. Trivia - Lily was friends with counter-culture icon Timothy Leary (who was an advocate of the therapeutic benefits of the mind-altering drug LSD). Timothy Leary was the godfather of Stranger Things star Winona Ryder.

(27)

Horror icon Robert Englund is in Stranger Things 4 as a killer named Victor Creel. Englund is of course best known for playing the razor-gloved Freddy Krueger eight times in The Nightmare on Elm Street series (plus Freddy vs Jason - where he squared off with Crystal Lake's infamous hockey mask wearing lunatic Jason Vorhees).

Englund was born in 1947 and studied classical theatre at acting school. He had early dreams of being a very serious actor. His initial roles were modest and patchy though, including a bit part in the cult surfing film Big Wednesday and an appearance in Roger Corman's largely forgotten but inventive low-budget Alien clone Galaxy of Terror. It was the V mini-series (where Englund played Willie, the kind alien who joined up with the human resistance) though that gave Englund his first experience of real fame.

V began life as a mini-series and quickly became a huge phenomenon. It was about a group of aliens arriving on Earth in huge flying saucer type crafts. They appear very human and friendly and establish good relations. It's all a front though. They are lizards wearing human masks and intent on pillaging the Earth and using us as food. The aliens (or 'visitors') are basically the Nazis. They have fascist uniforms and symbols and set up a youth movement. Humans are encouraged to collaborate and spy on trouble makers.

V was a huge hit when it first aired and A Nightmare On Elm

Street soon followed. Freddy Krueger became hugely popular, a cult film monster not too far off Dracula and The Mummy in terms of fame. It's slightly odd that Freddy was supposed to be a child killer who was murdered and now spends his time bumping off teenagers but ended up with a range of toy dolls and a young fanbase! Englund would have to endure marathon sessions in the make-up chair each time he played Freddy Krueger (Freddy's scarred face resembled the melted cheese on a well done pizza).

Englund has also appeared on a huge amount of television shows. Babylon 5, MacGyver, Walker: Texas Ranger, Masters of Horror, Sliders, Knight Rider, Charmed, and many more. He's also quite a dab hand at voicing villains in cartoons and has been both The Riddler and The Vulture in Justice League, Spider-Man, and Batman animations.

(28)

The first season of Stranger Things attracted over 14 million viewers in its first 35 days online.

(29)

Gaten Matarazzo said he tried to buy a Dungeons & Dragons set when he was cast in Stranger Things but he couldn't find one in the shops anywhere and had to resort to eBay.

(30)

Mike Wheeler is the first character in Stranger Things to use the term the Upside Down.

(31)

Finn Wolfhard said that when production began on the first season of Stranger Things he was so excited to be there he literally didn't stop talking for weeks. Finn said he liked the concept of Stranger Things so much he would happily have played any role in the show.

(32)

The makeup department on Stranger Things 3 complained when the catering department served the cast freeze-pops during a warm spell. Freeze-pops are a nightmare for the makeup people and continuity because all the actors are liable to end up with orange or yellow tongues after eating them.

(33)

When the third season was released, an entertainment website complained that the subtitles for Stranger Things 3 made too much use of the words "squelching" and "squelch" in relation to the Flayer's body horror shenanigans. What words were they supposed to use?

(34)

Millie Bobby Brown said the worst thing about having extra short hair when she shot season one of Stranger Things was going out in the rain.

(35)

Gaten Matarazzo is not related to the actress Heather Matarazzo. Heather Matarazzo (who is best known for the films Welcome to the Dollhouse, The Princess Diaries, and Scream 3) once had to deny stories she was his mother. The confusion probably stemmed from the fact that Gaten's real mother is also named Heather.

(36)

Hallmark's Keepsake Ornament collection for the 2020 holiday season included a Demogorgon ornament designed for your Christmas tree.

(37)

Noah Schnapp said he was pleasantly surprised to be cast in Stranger Things because he didn't think his auditions were terribly good. Noah was away at summer camp when he got the news that he had been cast as Will Byers. While the rest of the cast were based in Atlanta for production on season one, Noah was slightly different because he commuted between his family home in New York and Atlanta. This was presumably a consequence of the fact that Will Byers is trapped in the Upside Down for much of season one so Noah had less scenes to shoot than the other kids.

When it came to season two, Noah was upgraded to full cast member and was based in Atlanta for the duration of the production. Noah said that on Stranger Things 2 he felt much more like a true part of the Stranger Things family.

(38)

Although she tends not to have much dialogue because Eleven is not the most verbose of characters, Millie Bobby Brown still has more overall actual screen time than any other actor in the show when the first three seasons of Stranger Things are all tallied together.

(39)

When it became available to stream, eighteen million people watched the whole of Stranger Things 3 inside four days.

(40)

Finn Wolfhard said he did not enjoy riding Mike Wheeler's bike in the first season because it was heavy and the gears were messed up. The bikes they used were not authentic 80s bikes but mash-ups constructed to LOOK like period BMX bikes. The reason why they couldn't source authentic 80s bikes is because they required so many for stand-ins, stunts, wear and tear, and stunt-doubles. Yes, even the kids in the first season had their own stunt doubles!

(41)

The Duffer Brothers said that they deliberately established in season one that Will Byers liked art and drawing because they knew that somewhere down the line (if Stranger Things got a second season) that Will would use art as a means to convey the nature of the Upside Down visions that plagued him.

(42)

When they have to depict blood in a character's mouth (or even near their mouth) in Stranger Things, the makeup department uses a fake blood mixture that is made up of dried cranberries, black cherry Jell-O mix, Emergen-C powder, and some water. Emergen-C is a powdered vitamin supplement. The most important thing is that it has to be safe to go inside the actor's mouth.

(43)

Netflix picked up over two million new subscribers in the third quarter of 2016. The spike in subscriptions was attributed to the positive buzz around Stranger Things.

(44)

Polish painter Zdzislaw Beksinski was an influence on the look of the Upside Down in Stranger Things. Beksinski's work was known for its nightmarish dystopian surrealism.

(45)

Gaten Matarazzo was the first of the kids to be cast in Stranger Things. Noah Schnapp was the last of the kids to be cast. The first adult to be cast was Winona Ryder. By casting Winona Ryder (who was obviously a big name thanks to her long movie career) the producers of Stranger Things were under less pressure to cast 'name' actors in other parts. From their point of view this was a very happy development. Actors like Joe Keery and even David Harbour were not especially famous at all but they were definitely right for the parts allocated to them.

(46)

Notice how Steve Harrington looks slightly baffled when Eleven returns at the end of the season two episode The Mind Flayer. This is because Steve has never met Eleven before.

(47)

The Demogorgon is one of the monsters in the classic 1983 Commodore 64 computer game Forbidden Forest. Forbidden Forest is an adventure/action game. The player is an archer who is in a forest full of monsters such as giant spiders, frogs, dragons, snakes and wizards. The final enemy is a Demogorgon. There are four difficulty levels: Innocent, Trooper, Daredevil and Crazy. The player has three lives and 40 arrows: they are refreshed at the end of each level. Level 1 involves huge black spiders. Level 2 has giant wasps. Level 3 has monster frogs. Level 4 has a dragon. Level 5 Ghosts and skeletons. Level 6 has a giant snake. Level 7 is the Demogorgon. If the player wins then the game starts with the next highest difficulty. Forbidden Forest is a very creepy and atmospheric game with scary monsters and a great horror style music score.

It is one of the earliest computer games to feature animated blood. The graphics are rudimentary and blocky but they add to the charm. They are almost in the style of an abstract art painting - adding to the surreal atmosphere of the game. Also, the game has parallax scrolling, a day night cycle and some of the monsters move forward from the background. This is, despite its fairly ordinary looking graphics, a very groundbreaking cinematic game for 1983.

The programmer Paul Norman wanted to create a cinematic style experience and his monsters were inspired by the films Night of the Demon (1957), Jason and the Argonauts (1983) and Mysterious Island (1961). Norman had nearly finished the game when the company he was working for Synchro went out of business. Luckily another company - Cosmi - hired him after they saw Forbidden Forest and he was able to complete the game.

(48)

Dungeons & Dragons, the board game which features so heavily in the first season of Stranger Things, became caught up in what became known as the Satanic Panic. Religious and parent groups claimed that the game was turning children into Devil worshippers! In 1982, a young man named Irving Pulling shot himself and his family blamed his obsession with Dungeons & Dragons. An organisation called B.A.D.D. (Bothered About Dungeons & Dragons) and Christian groups tried to get the game banned because they believed it celebrated demonology and witchcraft. The game was even banned from a few school libraries in America as a consequence.

In 1979, 16-year-old child prodigy James Dallas Egbert III vanished from his room at Michigan State University. He was later found in tunnels underneath the university. Egbert, who had mental health problems, later shot himself. His disappearance and later death was all blamed on Dungeons & Dragons. The moral panic over Dungeons & Dragons got so bizarre in the end there were even stories about participants in the game seeking to heighten the experience by having Dungeons & Dragons sessions in caves and underground catacombs and then vanishing - never to be seen again.

The fact that anyone believed your average Dungeons & Dragons player was a Devil worshipping occultist who spent their spare time lurking in caves and catacombs was a bit ridiculous to say the least.

(49)

In 2015, Finn Wolfhard was cast as Richie Tozier in a film version of Stephen King's IT. Finn was cast by Cary Fukunaga - who was slated to direct IT at the time. Cary Fukunaga then left the production of IT and had be replaced by another director. This meant there was a delay and during that period Finn took part in open auditions for Stranger Things. Had there not been a change of director and delay in the production of IT then Finn would never have been cast as Mike Wheeler in Stranger Things because he simply wouldn't have been available. Cary Fukunaga was eventually replaced by Andy Muschietti as the director of IT. Finn actually had to audition again for Muschietti but it went well and for the second (and thankfully final) time he was given the part of Richie Tozier.

Stephen King's IT was a story the Duffer Brothers had always wanted to turn into a film themselves. It was a complete coincidence that Finn was cast in two such similar projects around the same time. Finn said that because Mike in Stranger Things and Richie in Stephen King's IT are very different characters, it was a fun acting challenge to play both roles around the same time. Finn later shot Stranger Things 3 and his contribution to the IT sequel at the same time. He said this was rather taxing but enjoyable all the same.

(50)

The first season of Stranger Things, in terms of its concept, is rather reminiscent of a 1963 Richard Matheson penned Twilight Zone episode called Little Girl Lost. What is the premise of Little Girl Lost? When his daughter Tina (Tracy Stratford) rolls under her bed one night and vanishes, Chris Miller (Robert Sampson) is bewildered as he can hear her calling out from somewhere in the room but can't find Tina anywhere. Equally strange is the fact that the family dog bolted after Tina under the bed and disappeared too. Chris and his wife Ruth (Sarah Marshall) summon family friend and physicist Bill (Charles Aidman) for help with this puzzling mystery and Bill listens to the distant cries (and barks!) for help and comes to a remarkable conclusion. He believes Tina has fallen through a hole into another dimension. The gateway must be somewhere near her bed. Will it be possible to follow Tina there and bring her safely back to our own reality?

(51)

Gaten Matarazzo originally auditioned to play Mike Wheeler in Stranger Things. He also read for the part of Lucas Sinclair. Gaten said that when he did his audition he actually read the lines intended for Lucas because there was hardly any dialogue for Dustin. Dustin Henderson was a pretty vague character at the time - at least until Gaten was cast. Gaten said that when he was cast in Stranger hings he had to keep it a secret and was only allowed to tell his immediate family.

(52)

One thing that really helped to get Stranger Things into production (after a frustrating raft of early rejections) was Shawn Levy. Levy, a director, producer, and writer best known for films like the Night at the Museum series and Real Steel, encountered the pitch and story treatment for Montauk and loved the concept. He became a director and producer on Stranger Things and a tireless champion for the project.

Rightly or wrongly, Levy was seen as a director of forgettable mainstream comedies (his movies include family comedy Cheaper by the Dozen and the much derided 'new' version of The Pink Panther where Steve Martin replaced the irreplaceable Peter Sellers). His work on Stranger Things showed though that Levy had a good eye for horror and science fiction.

(53)

The number of people playing Dungeons & Dragons at home

surged by over 20% during the worldwide pandemic and lockdowns.

(54)

Over 800,000 people watched the whole of Stranger Things 3 within 24 hours of its release.

(55)

The Duffer Brothers said that they vaguely considered pitching Montauk as an anthology show (where each season would have different characters) at one point but were never convinced this was the right approach so quickly went off the idea. The anthology format of the type the Duffers considered has become quite common in modern television through shows like Fargo, American Horror Story, and True Detective.

(56)

On the first ever day of shooting on Stranger Things the boys all got the giggles because Finn Wolfhard sneezed during a take.

(57)

Dacre Montgomery, rather effectively, also did the voice for the evil Flayed version of Billy in season three. It's a very good piece of voice acting.

(58)

Netflix gave the go ahead for Stranger Things 2 before the first season had even been released. This was not officially announced though until a month after the first season came out. Although the Duffer Brothers had already started writing season two during this period they were not allowed to tell anyone.

(59)

Roads named Mt. Sinai, Cornwallis, and Kerley in Stranger Things are references to real places in North Carolina where the Duffer Brothers were raised.

(60)

The character of Mike Wheeler was originally going to have a large birthmark on his face but they didn't do this in the end.

(61)

The five stages of Demogorgon development are Pollywog, Frogogorgon, Catogorgon, Demodog, and Demogorgon.

(62)

Although it is a very old game now, statistics suggest that 40% of the people who play Dungeons & Dragons are under the age of 25.

(63)

Nancy has a classmate called Ally in season one. This could be a reference to Ally Sheedy of The Breakfast Club fame.

(64)

Synth music is a subgenre of new wave music that features the synthesizer as the dominant musical instrument. This type of music had its roots in the 1960s and 1970s. Synth music is a big part of the Stranger Things score.

(65)

Stranger Things was originally titled Montauk. Montauk is a hamlet at the east end of the Long Island peninsula and famed for its beaches. Ross and Matt Duffer, the brothers who created Stranger Things, were very inspired by Steven Spielberg's classic movie Jaws in their early plans for the show. One of the main reasons why the show was originally going to be set in Montauk is Camp Hero. Camp Hero (aka Montauk Air Force Station) is an abandoned military base in Montauk which gave rise to all manner of conspiracy theories. It was alleged in a book called The Montauk Project that Camp Hero used kidnapped children in experiments which included telekinesis and time travel. Most of the conspiracy theories involving Montauk are obviously considered to be fiction but the Duffers felt Camp Hero (with its many urban legends and alleged secrets) would be a great backdrop for a sci-fi fantasy horror show.

Most of the cast in Stranger Things were hired when the show was still going to be called Montauk. Montauk was eventually dropped as the location for the show because the Duffers, upon reflection, decided a coastal shoot would present technical and logistical problems that were probably best avoided. The weather on the coast was an obvious concern. When the location of the show was changed this obviously meant it couldn't be called Montauk anymore. The Duffers said they had a terrible time trying to think of a new title for the show but eventually came up with Stranger Things.

(66)

The Duffers said that when the name of the show was changed from Montauk to Stranger Things they got a long email from David Harbour complaining about this change. David Harbour thought that Stranger Things was a terrible new title for the show. He said it took him a long time to get used to it.

(67)

Matt Duffer said it was him who came up with the idea to call the show Stranger Things after Montauk was axed. However, his brother Ross Duffer (like David Harbour) disliked Stranger Things as the new title. Matt Duffer got his way though and

Ross Duffer (like David Harbour) got used to the new title in the end.

(68)

Among the celebrities who say they enjoy playing Dungeons & Dragons are Joseph Gordon-Levitt, Vin Diesel, Stephen Colbert, and Jon Favreau.

(69)

The scene in Stranger Things 2 where Steve and Dustin gaze down the tunnel created by the escaped Dart is a homage to the scene in the 1994 film The Shawshank Redemption where the warden finds the tunnel in the wall that Andy Dufresne had dug to escape.

The Shawshank Redemption is based on a 1982 Stephen King novella called Rita Hayworth and Shawshank Redemption.

(70)

The Millennium Falcon toy that Eleven levitates in season one is the 1980 Empire Strikes Back Millennium Falcon reissue from Kenner Toys.

(71)

In the very early plans for Montauk, the Duffer Brothers briefly considered the show taking place in a frosty winter backdrop of snow and ice.

(72)

The sight of Eleven and Max in red and yellow raincoats when they arrive at Heather's house in The Case Of The Missing Lifeguard is very striking and evokes everything from Don't Look Now to the child twins in Kubrick's The Shining.

(73)

The term Demogorgon is believed to derive from a mistranslated of an old Greek manuscript.

(74)

Netflix picked up over six million new subscribers in the last quarter of 2017. The release of Stranger Things 2 was plainly the biggest factor in these new subscriptions.

(75)

The Duffer Brothers originally intended for only around 20% of the special effects in season one to be computer generated in order to replicate the old school practical FX eighties aesthetic of the films they loved (Evil Dead, Hellraiser, The Thing etc) and which inspired Stranger Things but in the end this proved unrealistic. Computer generated effects eventually accounted for about 50% of what you see in season one.

(76)

Netflix wanted season one of Stranger Things to have more than eight episodes but the Duffer Brothers chose not to do this because they wanted it to feel like one long movie. They sensibly didn't want the story to feel like it was being stretched out too thinly.

(77)

Gaten Matarazzo said his favourite character in Stranger Things is Murray Bauman and that he loves working with Brett Gelman.

(78)

The first season of Stranger Things appears to reference a Richard Matheson penned Twilight Zone episode called Mute.

Mute concerns a telepathic orphan girl who is taken in by a family with the surname Wheeler.

In the plot of Mute a group of people in Germany in the 1950s form a community that has developed telepathic powers and so have children that do not need to speak (as they obviously communicate through their mental powers). A family from the community moves to the United States but both parents are killed in a house fire. Their last act is to use their mental powers to warn and save their young telepathic mute daughter Ilse (Ann Jillian). The orphaned Ilse is taken in by Sheriff Harry Wheeler (Robert Boon) and his wife Cora (Barbara Baxley) while they try to locate any relatives she might have.

Not understanding the true nature of Ilse, the pair are appalled that she doesn't seem to be able to speak or read and enroll her in a school where a strict, insensitive and sadistic teacher named Edna Frank (Irene Dailey) becomes determined to make Ilse just like everyone else. While Sheriff Wheeler tries to make contact with any family the mute orphan might have in Germany, he is unaware that his wife is burning the letters and doing everything she can to make sure that Ilse never leaves. Their own daughter drowned in an accident and Cora is maniacally determined to maintain possession of Ilse - who she is irrationally believes is her own daughter somehow returned to her. In the middle of all of this is Ilse, marooned, alone and isolated in her own mind, and unable to communicate with anyone.

You could say that Ilse shares a number of similarities with the character of Eleven. They both have uncanny powers and don't speak much.

(79)

The boys in Stranger Things had to perform a specific scene from E.T as part of their auditions. The scene in question was when Eliott is about to show his brother E.T for the first time.

(80)

Matt Duffer said that when you audition children for acting roles you can tell in seconds if they are any good or not.

(81)

The Duffer Brothers said they first started making little home movies together when they were in the third grade.

(82)

Stranger Things never really pinpoints where exactly in Indiana the town of Hawkins is located. One of the spin-off novels seems to place it near Bloomington.

(83)

The acronym for Hawkins Power and Light, the cover name for the secret government agency meddling with the Upside Down, is HPL. This is a reference to the famous horror author H.P. Lovecraft.

Lovecraft's stories are often about inexplicable creatures, alternate dimensions, and forces we can't possibly understand. His work was a big influence on Stranger Things - especially his story From Beyond. From Beyond (which spawned a decent 1986 film adaptation by Stuart Gordon) is told from the perspective of a narrator and spins the ghastly yarn of a scientist named Crawford Tillinghast. Tillinghast invents a gadget that affects the pineal gland and allows one to see dimensions and planes of existence beyond our own reality.

Lovecraft's most famous story is At the Mountains of Madness, first published in 1936. The story is set in the lonely windswept interior of the Antarctic plateau and told by Professor William Dyer - a geologist from Miskatonic University. Dyer's terrible tale is a warning to a planned scientific expedition of Antarctica not to travel to this frozen outpost and follow in his footsteps. He led a team of scholars from Miskatonic University there to extract geological and biological specimens but what they found was so horrifying that his official report had to be censored. Ancient pre-human alien life forms, a lost city, biological engineers who dissect humans for experimentation, creatures so indescribably hideous that one look at them would lead to insanity. As if this all wasn't bad enough, there were also (gulp) giant penguins.

(84)

When we see a lab scientist enter the Upside Down in season one but he doesn't survive for very long. The doomed scientist is called Shephard. Shephard is the name of a character in Silent Hill and also the 1984 horror film C.H.U.D. In this specific case though it could be a reference to Alan Shepard - the first American in space.

(85)

For the climax of The Spy, Will informs the scientists of where he thinks the Mind Flayer is hiding and they send soldiers scurrying into the tunnels. An unapologetic and hugely enjoyable homage to the sequence in James Cameron's Aliens where the Colonial Marines are ambushed by the acid blooded monsters is the end result.

(86)

Because the walls in the Byers house had to be constantly trashed or graffited in season one, the production team came up with the clever idea of printing the wallpaper pattern onto latex for whenever they needed a fresh wall.

(87)

David Harbour insisted on Hopper having a cut lip in Stranger Things 3 but this proved to be a pain for the makeup department because everytime he had his lunch the lip cut makeup effect would be ruined by him eating food.

(88)

One of the many monster influences on the Demogorgon was the Pale Man (aka Eyeball Hands) in Pan's Labrynth.

(89)

There seem to be some Catcher in the Rye references in Stranger Things. The Catcher in the Rye is a 1951 novel by J. D Salinger.

The first reference comes during the memorial to Will Byers in the school in season one when Mike calls some of the people who have (despite hardly knowing Will) turned up 'phonies' - a term that Holden Caulfield uses frequently in Catcher in the Rye.

In season two there seems to be another Catcher reference when Eleven is a fugitive in the woods and has a hunting hat she took from a hunter. Holden wears a red hunting hat in the book, which he turns backwards. The hat has many possible meanings. His younger siblings Allie and Phoebe had red hair so it represents a connection to their innocence for Holden (who complains about his own white hairs despite his young age). The hat looks like baseball headgear backwards - an obvious link with a catcher. Hunters also wear red hats for protection, another possible link. When Holden is happy to let the hat go it suggests he no longer clings to fantasies of being a catcher in the rye and preserving innocence forever.

(90)

Gaten Matarazzo has a condition called cleidocranial dysplasia - a rare disorder that affects the growth of bones and teeth. Gaten's cleidocranial dysplasia was written into his character Dustin Henderson in Stranger Things. Gaten has campaigned to raise awareness of cleidocranial dysplasia. He says that many sufferers have worse cases of the condition than he does. Gaten said that, happily, his cleidocranial dysplasia hasn't really hindered his acting career too much - though it did complicate it somewhat in the early days. Gaten's sister said that his agent didn't think Gaten would get any television work because of he had a slight lisp at the time. Happily the agent was wrong about that. It was Gaten's idea for his character Dustin Henderson to have cleidocranial dysplasia. He felt it would help raise awareness for the condition.

Because of his cleidocranial dysplasia, Gaten wears dentures in Stranger Things.

(91)

Shannon Purser was working in a cinema and had no professional acting experience when she was cast as Barbara 'Barb' Holland in season one.

(92)

Stranger Things makeup department head Amy L. Forsythe said that for the infection wounds in season three she researched the effect of animal bites on human skin and then replicated this with the use of mannequin legs to refine the makeup effects. Amy said she got some rather bemused and baffled looks from her team at first when she asked them to go out and buy her some mannequins.

(93)

Gaten Matarazzo said he asked for Dustin to have a dog in Stranger Things 2 but the Duffers gave Dustin an Upside Down creature as a pet instead.

(94)

70% of viewers who watched up to the second episode of Stranger Things went on to view the whole first season.

(95)

The Duffer Brothers and Shawn Levy said they had a marathon three hour meeting with Winona Ryder when they were trying to persuade her to sign up to Stranger Things.

(96)

Shooting Stranger Things 4 was quite complex because of the pandemic protocols. The cast had to wear masks on the set and be separated during lunch.

(97)

Finn Wolfhard said the kiss between Mike and Eleven in the season one finale of Stranger Things wasn't his first kiss because he kissed a girl when he was in kindergarten. Millie Bobby Brown teased him about this and said he was probably making that kindergarten story up.

(98)

The term "Slurpee" comes from the slurping sound this beverage makes when it is consumed through a straw. A man named Omar Knedlik is generally credited with inventing this drink - though by accident. When his soda fountain malfunctioned, Knedlik put some soda in the freezer and they became festooned with ice. The references to 'Slurpees' in Stranger Things 3 probably derive from the cult Winona Ryder film Heathers. In that film Winona's character was a fan of cherry Slurpees.

(99)

When the character of Will Byers is possessed by the Upside Down in Stranger Things 2, the makeup department used special effects contacts to make Noah Schnapp's eyes look much darker. They obviously needed Will to look much more sinister and otherworldly than his usual innocent self.

(100)

The monster in season three was partly inspired by Frankenstein because they wanted it to feel like it was constructed of various different body parts and a disconcerting patchwork of gore.

Frankenstein is a novella written by Mary Shelley when she was only eighteen years-old. Frankenstein is a pioneering work of science fiction and an enduring touchstone of horror. To this day, rarely a year goes past without a film that was inspired by Frankenstein going into production. It is hard to think of any work of fiction that has been as influential as Frankenstein was to the horror genre. The book was written in 1818 while Mary was staying a villa near Geneva close to Lord Byron. The story was, appropriately enough, inspired by a nightmare.

The story in Frankenstein is told through the letters of an explorer named Captain Robert Walton. Walton is on an exploration of the North Pole and runs into a mysterious and cultivated Swiss scientist named Victor Frankenstein. Frankenstein has discovered a way to bring life to body parts that were previously dead. He has meddled with things that shouldn't really have been meddled with at all. The end result is the creation of a monster who inspires fear but only wants to be loved and accepted. We are faced with the realisation that the real monster may not be this unfortunate creature but Victor Frankenstein himself. Even if you've never read Frankenstein before you might feel as if you are already familiar with this story. The mad scientist, a lightning crackled Gothic laboratory, villagers with pitchforks and flaming torches. However, if that's the case you will be surprised at how the original novel subverts your expectations.

This book is a lot different to how one might expect it to be from watching Frankenstein movies. The story is more complex, much bigger, more nuanced, and simply a lot more surprising than any film version you might have seen. As a consequence, Frankenstein feels like a fresh and novel experience which is completely different to what you expected. Frankenstein is one of the true landmarks and cornerstones of the horror genre but also a very moving and very human story.

(101)

Project MKUltra features heavily in season one of Stranger Things. From 1953 to 1973, the CIA funded experiments in order to learn how to control people for the purposes of spying. These experiments were designed to see if the human mind could be altered or controlled. The psychedelic drug LSD was a big part of the experiments and sensory deprivation chambers were used.

The origins of the project are thought to have come from a fear that the Soviet Union was much more advanced in brainwashing techniques. This was a sphere of the Cold War that America was apparently losing and so was born (after several similar if smaller projects) MKUltra. For the CIA, the worst-case scenario was that the Soviet Union could find a way to mindcontrol US military and intelligence officials.

It all sounds somewhat crazy and fantastical but experiments in psychological techniques were very real. The experiments included attempts to 'remote control' people for the purposes of manipulating agents in the field through electrical brain triggers.

Obviously, the concept of anyone gaining super powers through MKUltra experiments is pure fantasy though. Project MKUltra ended in 1973 and only became public knowledge after the experiment was terminated.

(102)

Mike and Eleven in Stranger Things are known as Mileven by fans because of their romance.

(103)

Stranger Things 3 was viewed by more than 60 million member households in its first month. This was a record for a Netflix show.

(104)

The kids in Stranger Things like to decorate their trailers when a new season is in production.

(105)

There were whispers before Stranger Things 3 that Mike Wheeler was going to be killed off because Finn Wolfhard was too busy to be in the show anymore. This turned out to be complete nonsense. For some reason there always seems to be speculation before any new season of Stranger Things that Jonathan Byers is going to be killed off. This is not though something that (to the great relief of Charlie Heaton and his bank manager you'd imagine) was ever on the cards.

(106)

Millie Bobby Brown only has forty-two lines as Eleven in the whole of season one. Millie said that when she turned up on the set and actually had a line to say it felt like Christmas. Millie added that it was all rather ironic because she is very good at learning lines and actually enjoys this part of being an actor.

(107)

A survey in 2017 found 31% of young adults had watched all the episodes of Stranger Things. Another 17% of respondents said they had seen at least some of the show and intended to watch more in the future. The survey suggested that 57% of Stranger Things viewers are female.

(108)

Gaten Matarazzo said he only knew for sure that Hopper would be in Stranger Things 4 when he saw David Harbour at the table read for the new season.

(109)

The makeup department used lip gloss on Dacre Montgomery to make Billy Hargrove appear hot and sweaty in the sauna sequence in Stranger Things 3. The specific brand they used was M.A.C. clear Lipglass.

(110)

In the original plan for Montauk (later to become Stranger Things), the school science teacher Mr Clarke was going to be one of the main characters and at the heart of the story, action, and intrigue. The original conception the Duffers had for Mr Clarke was essentially for him to be like the Indiana Jones of Hawkins. In the end the character of Mr Clarke was radically altered in the transition from pitch to final product. No longer was Mr Clarke the dashing hero saving the kids but now more of a lovably nerdy comic background character who isn't even aware of the strange things happening in Hawkins.

It could be that the Duffers, after mulling it over, felt that by having Mr Clarke as an Indiana Jones type character solving all the mysteries this would dilute the other characters in the show and make them feel less necessary.

(111)

The small town of Jackson in Georgia often doubles for (the obviously fictional) Hawkins in Stranger Things. Jackson is nearly fifty miles from the heart of Atlanta and has a population of around 5,000. Those with cafes or stores in Jackson have enjoyed the financial perks of Stranger Things tourists visiting the town. You could probably describe

Jackson as a commuter town given its relative proximity to Atlanta. The Town Square of Mulberry Street in Jackson is used the most for shooting in Stranger Things.

(112)

Steve Harrington and Eleven were both originally going to be killed off in the original plan for season one. This would obviously have been a mistake as they are arguably the two most popular characters in the show now.

Steve Harrington was originally conceived as just your basic teen villain but the Duffers like Joe Keery so much they decided to keep Steve in the show and give him a redemptive story (as opposed to him just being a straight up teen baddie). It could be that the Duffers rather miscast Keery as the villain in season one because Keery is a funny and likable sort of actor - even as a villain. It made sense then to turn Steve Harrington into one of the heroes and thus play to Keery's strengths much more.

Dacre Montgomery as Billy in season two is more like what Steve was supposed to be like in the early plans for the show.

As for Eleven, the original plan was that Eleven sacrifices herself saving the boys in the finale and that was the end of her arc. At the time the Duffers had no way of knowing if Stranger Things was going to be popular or have further seasons. In a sense, if season one was all we ever got of Stranger Things and so was sort of like a miniseries, then Eleven's death would probably work from a dramatic point of view. However, when Millie Bobby Brown turned in an amazing performance and became the breakout star of the show and Stranger Things was a fairly instant phenomenon then the thought of killing Eleven off for good suddenly became unthinkable.

People would have been dreadfully disappointed if Eleven wasn't in Stranger Things 2.

(113)

The Starcourt Mall in Stranger Things 3 is really Gwinnett Place Mall in Atlanta. This mall opened in 1984 but eventually fell on hard times and was pretty derelict when the Stranger Things production team found it. Netflix leased about 20% of the mall and completely renovated it - putting in the facades of around forty 1980s period authentic stores. They also installed an operational food court.

Stranger Things staff writer Kate Trefry is believed to have been the person who came up with the idea of a mall opening in Hawkins. The Duffers liked this idea because they grew up in an area with three malls and had happy memories of being 'mall rats' themselves. Malls were a very big thing in the 1980s but although they still exist today the advent of online shopping has made it more difficult for them to thrive in the way they used to.

The Duffers asked production designer Chris Trujillo to include Scoops Ahoy (inspired by Baskin-Robbins) and Gap in the mall but said the rest of the stores were up to him. The final list of stores at the Starcourt Mall is The Gap, Sam Goody, Waldenbooks, Claire's, Zales, RadioShack, Kaufman Shoes, Jazzercise, Wicks 'N' Sticks, Regis Hairstylists, Lovelace Lingerie, Fine Perfumes, Camera Repair, JCPenney, JCPenney Home Store, SHAPES Activewear Outlet, The Game Player, Chess King, The Eyewear House, ESPRIT - Coming Soon, Spencer's Gifts - Coming Soon, Scoops Ahoy, Hot Dog on a Stick, The Great Cookie, Teppanyaki, New York Pizza, Orange Julius, Burger King, Hawkins' Heroes, Hot Sam Pretzels, Imperial Panda, The Nut Shack, Wyatt's Cafeteria, The Ground Round, Taco Bell - Coming Soon, Starcourt Cinemas, Time-Out Arcade, Flash Studio.

It took a production team of eighty people six weeks to turn a derelict corner of Gwinnett Place Mall into a realistic facsimile of a functioning 1985 mall.

(114)

The store where Eleven steals the waffles in season one is really Bradley's Big Buy grocery store (now part of the Piggly Wiggly franchise) in Palmetto, Georgia. The owner of this store said that their sales of Eggo waffles usually treble when a new season of Stranger Things comes out.

(115)

Caleb McLaughlin, Sadie Sink, and Gaten Matarazzo all vaguely knew each other before Stranger Things because they had worked on Broadway and the stage and their paths had crossed. Gabriella Pizzolo, who plays Dustin's girlfriend Suzie in Stranger Things 3, also has a Broadway background. These stage kids are obviously good at acting auditions.

(116)

The real shooting location for the cinema in Hawkins is 12 Oak Street, Jackson, Georgia. The building used is a furniture store which has its exterior altered to look like the outside of a cinema. In the original plan for Stranger Things the character of Jonathan Byers was going to work in this cinema but they obviously decided not to do this in the end.

(117)

Though he hosts his own Netflix prank show, Gaten Matarazzo says that Millie Bobby Brown and Noah Schnapp are the biggest pranksters on the set of Stranger Things.

(118)

The special effects in season one in particular of Stranger Things are hugely impressive because the budgets and time allocated to the FX departments were not remarkable by television standards. The Demogorgon was a mixture of practical and digital effects in season one. When the creature battles the boys and Eleven at the end of season one this is a digital effect but for the most part in season one the monster was played by Mark Steger in a suit. It took half an hour for Steger to get into the suit and the elongated arms were operated by puppeteers. Designing the Demogorgon was a long process. There were test models of the creature that took over a month to construct.

Unused concepts for the Demogorgon included the idea of making it more Swamp Thing in design and covering the creature in moss and tree bark.

(119)

In season one of Stranger Things, Mike compares Dustin's cleidocranial dysplasia to having a superpower and mentions Mr Fantastic of Fantastic Four fame. Everyone probably knows who the Fantastic Four are by now.

Four astronauts are bombarded with uncanny cosmic rays in space when they test their experimental rocket. They return to Earth and realise they now have remarkable and very strange powers that take some getting used to. Brilliant scientist/inventor and Fantastic Four leader Reed Richards can now stretch his body like a piece of elastic and becomes known as Mr Fantastic. Sue Storm (Reed's girlfriend) can now make herself invisible (and is later able to generate force fields) and becomes Invisible Girl. Johnny Storm (Sue's brother) now has the ability to control fire and fly and becomes the Human Torch while the last member of the team Ben Grimm has his body turned into formidable orange rock (no idea why they made it orange but it looks good!) and becomes the Thing.

The four adopt blue costumes (well, three of them do anyway) and become The Fantastic Four, using their powers and scientific knowledge for good and vanquishing Earth threatening villains who have cosmic carnage up their galaxy spanning sleeves. This was a new type of comic in many ways at the time and became popular and famous for these irreverent qualities although the characters are largely great too of course. The four central protagonists of Fantastic Four were not stoic square jawed superheroes with no flaws but very human and like a big dysfunctional family. They argued and bickered a lot and the comic was notable for its sense of humour.

The Fantastic Four were somewhat radical in the way that they made no attempt to hide their identity and instead embraced their celebrity status. They didn't wear masks or have a secret headquarters. The Fantastic Four were an open book and would appear on television or do interviews. It was a nice premise and made for some good jokes. I like the fact that the team are quite self-deprecating too. Bickering superhero teams are nothing out of the ordinary now but it was a departure at the time. Stan Lee's approach was to make his heroes more flawed than the DC ones and also more bizarre. People who had got their powers from strange scientific accidents rather than being born with them. Pseudo-science superpowered troubleshooters.

(120)

Stephen King is obviously a huge influence on Stranger Things. King's path to becoming a one-man book industry was remarkable in its origins. He was a teacher living in a mobile home and doing a shift in a laundry. He started writing a book called Carrie and was so dismayed by the results of his labour he threw it in a dustbin. His wife Tabitha fished it out and persuaded him to stick at it. Carrie eventually sold for $400,000 and King was soon a phenomenon in terms of book sales.

(121)

When she first became an actor, Millie Bobby Brown was billed simply as Millie Brown. She then added 'Bobby' to her name as a way to avoid confusion with a controversial performance artist named Millie Brown. These days though Millie's fame far outstrips that of the performance artist who shares her name.

(122)

There was a Dungeons & Dragons cartoon which ran from 1983 to 1985 on the CBS network. You can hear a snatch of the music from this cartoon in Stranger Things 3 when Hopper and Joyce arrive at the fair. The characters in the cartoon were Hank (The Ranger), Eric (The Cavalier), Diana (The Acrobat), Presto (The Magician), Sheila (The Thief), Bobby (The Barbarian), Uni (The Unicorn), and Dungeon Master.

(123)

Shannon Purser filmed her Stranger Things audition tape in the basement of her parents' home.

(124)

Michael Stein and Kyle Dixon of the electronic synth group Survive (S U R V I V E) were chosen to compose the score for Stranger Things. The Duffers were impressed by their work on the offbeat 2014 thriller film The Guest.

(125)

Notice how the music score stops and there is silence during the big van flip stunt in The Bathtub. This tactic by the composers is very effective.

(126)

The Duffer Brothers said that they made Noah Schnapp do some emotional scenes at his first auditions because they already had a long term plan for a future season where Will Byers would be possessed by the Upside Down. They needed to make sure that the child they cast as Will Byers would be capable of playing this storyline in the future.

(127)

Billy Hargrove was supposed to play a much bigger part in Stranger Things 2 but there wasn't room for this in the end. The Duffer Brothers said that Billy's 'teen supernatural' storyline got booted into season three instead.

(128)

Holly Wheeler is deliberately made to look like Drew Barrymore's Gertie from E.T. in season one.

(129)

Millie Bobby Brown said the other kids in the Stranger Things cast helped her to get her American accent right when she played Eleven.

(130)

You could say that Stranger Things 3 is the 'Red Scare' season of the show, drawing some influences from the likes of The Manchurian Candidate, Indiana Jones and the Kingdom of the Crystal Skull, Red Dawn, and Rocky IV (in the cartoonish portrayal of the dastardly Soviets).

Classic monster movies where the monster could be interpreted as a manifestation of Soviet communism include The Blob (a clear influence in Stranger Things 3), 1954's Them! (a classic black and white monster film about giant radiated, mutated ants running amok in the New Mexico desert), 1956's Earth vs. the Flying Saucers, and John Carpenter's The Thing.

(131)

The slogan "L'eggo My Eggo" was first coined in 1972. A real commercial featuring this phrase was used as part of the Stranger Things 2 teaser trailer. The commercial featured two children - one of whom was Jason Hervey. Hervey later played Wayne Arnold on the popular television show The Wonder Years.

(132)

The Duffer Brothers said their main objective with the casting in season one was to cast kids and actors who felt like real people.

(133)

Millie Bobby Brown said she wasn't too phased by the fact that Eleven is a very nonverbal sort of role (especially in season one). Millie said it was a fun and interesting challenge to have to largely act with her face rather than through dialogue.

(134)

Gaten Matarazzo said he especially liked making Stranger Things 4 because he was legally no longer a minor and so there were no longer any restrictions on what hours or times he could work anymore. Gaten loves night shoots so this was a definite plus as far as he was concerned.

(135)

Noah Schnapp as Will Byers had the thirteenth most amount of screentime of any character in season one. This lowly position was obviously because Will spent most of season one trapped in the Upside Down.

In season two though Noah ranked fourth when it came to screentime thanks to the major storyline involving the possessed Will Byers. When it came to season three, Noah ranked only tenth in terms of screentime. They didn't seem to find much for Will Byers to do in Stranger Things 3.

(136)

New Coke features in Stranger Things 3. In 1985 the popular beverage Cocoa-Cola was rebranded as New Coke and had its taste altered. The general theory behind the change seems to be that Coke was losing the sales battle with Pepsi at the time so decided to make Cocoa-Cola sweeter to compete with Pepsi. Well, as you probably know, there were a lot of protests at the change and after about six months later they got rid of New Coke and brought back the original Cocoa-Cola. New Coke was released again in 2019 in a marketing tie-in with Stranger Things 3 and the demand was so great the Cocoa-Cola website crashed.

It was rather ironic that New Coke - regarded to be one of the great marketing disasters in history - was now popular enough to crash a website! People were simply curious to learn what it tasted like.

(137)

Stranger Things editor Dean Zimmerman said he loves watching Stranger Things episode reaction videos on YouTube. Zimmerman said that he finds it emotional to see how much people love the show.

(138)

The Duffer Brothers say that on Stranger Things they are very aware of the need to alleviate the tension and horror with comedy. This is probably why Stranger Things is so appealing. It's a fun watch - as opposed to something that is too grim and takes itself too seriously.

(139)

In season one, when Nancy and Barb go to Steve's house party, the producers originally wanted to have AC/DC's Highway to Hell playing when Steve opens the door but they couldn't get the clearance to use the song.

(140)

The editors on Stranger Things said they got into the spirit of the show by decorating the screening room with 80s movie posters and Dungeons & Dragons stuff.

(141)

The production schedule on season one was that they had about twenty days to shoot each two episodes. Two episodes would be in production simultaneously.

(142)

The Duffers cut quite a lot of scenes out of the famous bike chase sequence in season one because they wanted it to be punchier and more fast paced.

(143)

The shoes worn by Noah Schnapp as Will Byers in season one were deliberately broken in and scuffed up to make it look like they were hand me downs from his brother Jonathan.

(144)

Finn Wolfhard as Mike Wheeler was given darker more subdued clothes in season two than season one to reflect his mood. Mike is rather sad in season two because of the loss of Eleven.

(145)

Finn Wolfhard, like his character Mike Wheeler, does actually play Dungeons & Dragons in real life. He said he acted as the gamesmaster for his former band. Finn said his dad played Dungeons & Dragons when he was a kid so was able to teach him about the game in preparation for playing Mike Wheeler in Stranger Things. Curiously, despite the importance of D&D to the plot of Stranger Things (especially the first season), the Duffer Brothers said that they never actually played this game themselves when they were children.

(146)

Even though they both work at Scoops Ahoy, you'll notice that Steve and Robin's uniforms are different. This is because the costume department thought that - visually - it might be a bit dull to watch two characters with the exact same costume.

(147)

Kyle Hill of Nerdist has speculated that the Upside Down could be the result of anomalous quantum waves and fluctuations - a quantum tapestry.

(149)

The early plan for the Upside Down was that it would exist in a completely different time zone from our own reality.

(150)

According to an article in Variety, the three biggest earners in Stranger Things 3 were Winona Ryder, David Harbour, and Millie Bobby Brown - who all made $350,000 an episode. The next tier of cast members (Natalia Dyer, Charlie Heaton, Gaten Matarazzo, Caleb McLaughlin, Finn Wolfhard, and Noah Schnapp) were all on a reported $250,000 an episode.

Millie Bobby Brown's alleged salary was especially impressive given that she was about fifteen at the time and yet still took home the same amount of money as the two adult leads in the show.

It was a far cry from season one - where Millie and kids were reportedly paid around $30,000 an episode.

(151)

Matthew Modine is the villain of the first season of Stranger Things as Dr Brenner (aka Papa to Eleven). Dr Brenner might be mean to Eleven but Millie Bobby Brown and Matthew Modine got on great. Millie said she had a nice family dinner with Matthew Modine during the shooting of season one.

(152)

Millie Bobby Brown said she shot a scene in season one where Eleven, while alone and exploring the Wheeler house while Mike is at school, reads some of Nancy's diary. This scene was cut though and did not appear onscreen.

(153)

Gaten Matarazzo said that Millie Bobby Brown was very shy when he first met her at the Stranger Things auditions.

(154)

The Duffer Brothers said that Mike Wheeler's name is a nod to Mikey Walsh in The Goonies. Sean Astin, who played Mikey Walsh, was part of the cast in Stranger Things 2. The Duffers were initially reluctant to cast Sean Astin as Bob Newby because they felt it would be too obvious (given the influence of The Goonies on Stranger Things) but they obviously changed their mind about this in the end. Astin had originally auditioned for the part of Murray Bauman but this role went to Brett Gelman.

On a trivia tangent, Astin has a connection to the Rob Reiner film Stand By Me - which is another huge influence on Stranger Things. Stand By Me is based on Stephen King's novella The Body (which inspired an episode title in season one of Stranger Things) and the child actors were asked to perform scenes from the movie when they auditioned for Stranger Things. Sean Astin tested for the part of Gordie Lachance in Stand By Me but this part eventually went to Wil Wheaton.

(155)

In the original pitch for Montauk, the first season was going to be set in 1980. The Duffers proposed that a second season would take place in 1990 - ten years later. The idea here was obviously that the kids would have to meet up again as young adults a decade later and fight the evil infecting Hawkins again. This was inspired by the structure of Stephen King's IT.

(156)

The first scene ever shot for Stranger Things was the first scene you see in the show - the Dungeons & Dragons game in Mike's basement. The Duffers wanted to put the boys together at the start of shooting because they wanted them to bond quickly - which thankfully did happen (the chemistry of the children is plain to see in season one). The kids said that when they were cast in Stranger Things they went to the cinema and amusement parks together as part of bonding exercises.

(157)

Caleb McLaughlin said he had to do five auditions before he got the part of Lucas Sinclair. Caleb said that he very nearly didn't turn up to the Montauk auditions though because at the time he had been rather bruised by a string of audition rejections and didn't really feel in the mood to go through this again.

In the original pitch for Montauk, Lucas was named Lucas Conley rather than Lucas Sinclair and was described as a 'comic relief' character who becomes increasingly troubled because of his parents divorce. Much of this was changed in the end. Caleb had a lot of input into the character of Lucas -

right down to the clothes. It was Caleb who came up with the idea of Lucas having a bandanna.

(158)

Before he turned his hand to acting, Charlie Heaton was the drummer in a rock band called Comanechi. He was then briefly in a psychedelic band called Half Loon. His early acting roles (aside from short films) were bit parts in the British television shows Vera, Casualty, and DCI Banks. Charlie said he fell into acting rather by accident. The drumming obviously wasn't paying the bills because he ran out of money in the end. He then signed up to a talent agency and began picking up acting jobs. He enjoyed these and so stuck with acting. Charlie said he had completely forgotten about his Stranger Things audition by the time the Duffers called him and said he had the part of Jonathan Byers.

(159)

When the third season became available to stream, nearly twenty million people watched the first episode inside 24 hours.

(160)

The introduction to Billy Hargrove in Stranger Things 2 mirrors that of the introduction to the school bully in the 1987 high school comedy film Three O'Clock High.

(161)

In the scene in season one where Eleven is in the sensory deprivation tank underwater in the Hawkins Lab, Millie Bobby Brown wore a real diving helmet that was equipped with a radio through which she could talk to the Duffer Brothers. They wanted to stay in constant communication with her just to make sure she was ok.

They also obviously needed a way to still direct her in the scene with instructions - despite Millie being underwater.

(162)

The Demogorgon made its first Dungeons & Dragons appearance in the 1976 game Eldritch Wizardry.

(163)

One problem they encountered with Atlanta as a production base for Stranger Things was shooting the Christmas scenes near the end of season one where it is supposed to be cold and frosty. Ice had to be imported in to make these scenes more authentic.

(164)

Sadie Sink said she had five callbacks during her audition process before she was cast as Maxine Mayfield in Stranger Things 2. A callback means that the director would like to see an actor again - perhaps to hear them read from the script or see them perform a scene next to another actor. Getting a callback doesn't automatically mean you have a part in the bag but if you keep getting called back this is obviously a good sign because it means they want to see you again.

(165)

Gaten Matarazzo said that secrecy measures to avoid spoilers on Stranger Things 2 became a bit paranoid in the end and everyone became worried there was a 'mole' in the crew leaking information! Gaten said that during production on season two he was banned from sending his brother any texts about the show lest he should let slip a spoiler.

(166)

The pairing of Steve and Dustin in Stranger Things 2 was more of a happy accident than anything planned out in advance. Weeks into the production on season two, the Duffers decided to put Dustin and Steve together for a few scenes as an experiment and found themselves instantly delighted by the comic chemistry between Gaten Matarazzo and Joe Keery. From that point on Steve and Dustin became a popular double-act in the show. Fans have even suggested we should get a Steve/Dustin spin-off show when Stranger Things ends. Gaten Matarazzo has said he would be up for this.

(167)

Kali has the number '8' on her wrist and was a victim of Brenner and the Hawkins Lab - like Eleven. Kali induces hallucinations and is a vigilante of sorts in the city. She tries to mentor Eleven and teach her how to focus on her powers. Kali is the name of a Hindu goddess. Kali is one of the ten Mahavidyas, a list which combines Sakta and Buddhist goddesses.

(168)

Steve Harrington has the fourth most amount of screentime of any character in season three. In the first two seasons he only ranked ninth and tenth respectively so Joe Keery enjoyed a much more expanded role in Stranger Things 3.

(169)

You could argue that there is a continuity error in season one because Eleven would appear to have escaped from the lab during the mayhem caused by her contact with the monster while in the water tank. However, Eleven is wearing a futuristic bathing suit during this scene but when we see her in The Vanishing of Will Byers for the first time she is wearing a hospital style gown.

Maybe she ditched the bathing suit and picked up a gown?

(170)

There is not a single episode in season one of Stranger Things where Finn Wolfhard as Mike Wheeler is not the top two when it comes to the most lines.

(171)

The shooting location for the Hawkins Public Library in Stranger Things is Butts County Probate Court, 3rd Street, Jackson, GA.

(172)

The costume department on season three were told to get rid of the plaid and browns of the clothes from the first two seasons and make the fashions in Stranger Things 3 more bold and vibrant.

Because the third season takes place in the summer they wanted the fashions to reflect that.

(173)

Brenner is a German-language surname. It originates from the Middle High German term "brennen", which means to burn.

(174)

Noah Schnapp contributed some of the crayon sketches that Will Byers does in season two to depict his experiences with the Flayer.

The crew did most of them though.

(175)

Stranger Things 4 is the first season of the show where we see Eleven attending school.

(176)

Priah Ferguson as Erica was promoted to main cast regular for Stranger Things 4.

(177)

Production on season four began in February 2020. However, the production was put on hold two weeks later because of the pandemic. Production only resumed again in September 2020. As a consequence of this fans would have to endure a long wait for season four. This was exacerbated by the fact that season four was more complex to shoot than previous seasons because it had more locations and a bigger scope.

(178)

There was speculation after season three that Stranger Things 4 would be the final season but this didn't turn out to be the case.

(179)

Some of season four was shot in the Lithuanian city of Vilnius at the 115 year-old Lukiškes Prison. This was closed as a real prison in 2019. Lukiškes Prison could hold 1,000 prisoners when it was still active.

(180)

Vilnius has become a popular location for TV shows to shoot in. Chernobyl, The Last Czars, Catherine the Great, and the BBC's War and Peace all did some shooting in Vilnius.

(181)

The Duffers were originally going to direct all of the episodes in season one but in order to give them time to finish the scripts for the final episodes Shawn Levy agreed to direct episodes three and four. This has become a tradition on the show - even a superstition you might say - and Shawn Levy now always directs the third and fourth episodes in each new season.

(182)

Gaten Matarazzo said it was something of a relief to finally finish shooting Stranger Things 4 because it had become a marathon production that went on forever.

(183)

In the comical indie RPG BoxxyQuest: The Gathering Storm, The Sky Queen character turns up late and explains this by saying she was busy binging Stranger Things.

(184)

The pilot script for Montauk was purchased by the production company 21 Laps - which was founded by Shawn Levy. It was Levy's idea to take the project to Netflix.

(185)

Matt Duffer said he got the idea to call the show Stranger Things because it sounded like the Stephen King title Needful Things.

(186)

When the Duffer Brothers were shopping around the Montauk idea they framed the pilot script with a home made cover which made use of the Stephen King book Firestarter.

(187)

The Demogorgon was designed to have a defined silhouette so that it would be a very unmistakable sort of monster.

(188)

The Duffer Brothers said that on a day shooting Stranger Things they usually have a couple of run throughs of the scenes - which act like rehearsals for the actors. Once the lighting is in place they will the go back and shoot those scenes for real.

(189)

The tunnels in season two were constructed on a sound-stage and amounted to 80,000 square feet. They decided not to use CGI for the tunnels because they wanted the actors to have a sense of real space and constriction - which made the performances more authentic. The strange Upside Down vines and flora of the tunnels were CGI though.

(190)

During the production of the episode The Weirdo on Maple Street, Millie Bobby Brown turned up for work one day with some gold glitter on her. Production was halted for half an hour while the glitter was removed.

(191)

Stranger Things 3 is the first season of the show where Will Byers appears in every episode.

(192)

The Hawkins Middle School Yearbook/Hawkins High School Yearbook is a book by Matthew J. Gilbert published by Penguin Random House.

The book contains a lot of trivia about the characters in Stranger Things. We learn, for example, that the full names of the school bullies Troy and James are Troy Walsh and James Dante.

(193)

Millie Bobby Brown said that her greatest crisis during season two came when she developed an annoying pimple on her ear! Happily, this pesky pimple was eventually vanquished.

(194)

In the pilot script for Montauk, the prologue in the lab (which in this case was Camp Hero) was much more gruesome than the prologue with the scientist in The Vanishing of Will Byers. In the pilot script we go straight into the aftermath of a massacre in the lab. The script describes headless and limbless dead scientists littered around the floor.

(195)

David Harbour said that on season one he found the scenes of Hopper in the Upside Down wearing a hazmat suit to be a complete pain because the suit took so long to get in and out of. Bathroom breaks were impossible.

(196)

The young actor Skylar Gaertner said he auditioned for two roles in Stranger Things but the producers never contacted him again after the auditions. It is believed that he probably tested for the parts of Mike Wheeler and Will Byers. Gaertner is best known now for his portrayal of Jonah Byrde in the Netflix drama Ozark.

(197)

The Duffer Brothers say that Stranger Things is not aimed at any age group. It is meant to be enjoyed by everyone. That could be why Networks passed on the show and didn't seem to get the concept. Maybe the Networks were puzzled as to whether this was a show for kids or adults. They didn't seem to understand that it was actually BOTH!

(198)

Dacre Montgomery had to spend up to five hours a day in the makeup chair to play the infected Billy Hargrove in Stranger Things 3.

(199)

In the pitch for Montauk, the character of Jonathan Byers investigates a curious dimensional rift that is left in the family shed after Will vanishes. This subplot never made it into Stranger Things.

(200)

Finn Wolfhard had to do some wire harness work for the scene in season one of Stranger Things where Mike jumps off the quarry ledge. It is said that the Duffers were dissatisfied with this sequence. The Duffers reportedly thought it looked too fake when Mike is levitated back up through the air by Eleven but there simply wasn't sufficient time or money to do this sequence all over again from scratch. Finn Wolfhard said the Duffer Brothers never told him that Eleven was going to save Mike so he initially thought his character was being killed off!

(201)

When the pandemic shut down production on Stranger Things 4, Gaten Matarazzo, who suddenly found himself at a loose end, volunteered as a food runner in a Long Beach Island restaurant. The place where Gaten worked as a food runner during the hiatus in production on Stranger Things 4 was Bird & Betty's on Long Beach Island. Gaten said he tried to go incognito with a hat but the customers knew it was him. Many people thought it was a bit weird that Gaten took a summer job in a diner when he has $4 million in the bank! Gaten said he simply wanted to do something constructive to kill time until production on Stranger Things began again. Maybe he was just bored.

(202)

Winona Ryder said she was attracted by Stranger Things because Joyce Byers was a very flawed and human sort of character. She also relished the chance to play someone her own age for a change. The Duffer Brothers said that Winona's name came up very early in the casting process in relation to Joyce and it was an idea they all loved.

(203)

David Harbour was pleasantly surprised to get the part of Jim Hopper in Stranger Things. Though he'd been around for quite a long period this was the first time that Harbour had been cast as a leading man in anything. Harbour only had to do one audition for Stranger Things (or Montauk as it would have been at the time). The Duffer Brothers said they decided to cast Harbour after watching him in a television drama called Manhattan. Manhattan ran from 2014 to 2015 and is about the development of the first atomic weapons. Harbour played a scientist in this show.

David Harbour partly based Hopper on Nick Nolte and Roy Scheider. Hopper is not a rippled six-pack stomach action hero but a plausible and flawed man who just happens to be very brave and determined.

(204)

The real shooting location for the Wheeler house in Stranger Things is Piney Wood Lane, East Point, Georgia 30344. Only the exteriors of the house are used though. The interior of the house you see in the show is a studio set. The Wheeler home was loosely inspired by the haunted house in Tobe Hooper's 1982 film Poltergeist. The composition of the Wheeler family also mirrors the Freeling family in Poltergeist in that the parents have an older daughter, middle son, and younger daughter.

(205)

Finn Wolfhard thought that dressing up as a Ghostbuster in Stranger Things 2 might preclude him from being in Ghostbusters: Afterlife but - happily - this wasn't the case.

(206)

Eleven had more screentime than any other character in the first two seasons. In season three though it is Hopper who has the most screentime.

(207)

In 2004, Wisconsin's Waupun Prison banned prisoners from playing Dungeons & Dragons because they claimed it promoted gang activity and cliques.

(208)

The Stranger Things youngsters were often seen at Six flags amusement park in Georgia when early seasons of Stranger Things were in production.

This theme park is only a twenty minute drive from Atlanta. Six flags amusement park now has a spooky Stranger Things maze.

(209)

In the pilot script for Montauk, Hopper's daughter Sarah died in a car accident.

(210)

David Harbour said that on season one of Stranger Things he isolated himself from the kids somewhat so that he could get into the detached headspace of Hopper.

(211)

Troy is the poisonous bully who makes life horrible for the boys at school in season one. Troy bites off more than he can chew though when he unwittingly runs into Mike's new friend Eleven. Eleven makes him wet himself and also snaps his arm at the quarry.

Peyton Wich, who played Troy, said he got on great with the Stranger Things kids in real life.

(212)

The Duffer Brothers said that directing together is fantastic because if one of them is tired or mentally frazzled on a particular day they can take a break and let the other one step in.

(213)

The name Mirkwood originally comes from a forest in Old Norse mythology. The source name is Myrkviðr - which means black forest. The boys in Stranger Things use Mirkwood as a name for a road and the area around the Hawkins National Laboratory.

(214)

Finn Wolfhard has joked that his Stranger Things co-stars always seem to know more about what is going to happen in the story than him.

(215)

The actual shooting location for the funeral of Will Byers in season one was Bethany Cemetery, Rivers Road, Fayetteville.

(216)

Finn Wolfhard said he was ordered to grow his hair long for Stranger Things 4.

(217)

Dacre Montgomery has said that the Duffers told him that Billy Hargrove was inspired by the possessed writer Jake Torrance in The Shining.

(218)

Millie Bobby Brown said she ate some mint tic tacs before she had to kiss Finn Wolfhard in the Stranger Things 2 finale.

(219)

Stranger Things was the subject of an affectionate Sesame Street parody in 2017.

(220)

Shawn Levy said that Winona Ryder constantly drank water in preparation for her crying scenes as Joyce in season one because she wanted to stay hydrated.

Apparently, drinking lots of water makes it easier to cry.

(221)

The Duffer Brothers blueprint for Stranger Things was 'Dark Amblin'. Amblin was Steven Spielberg's company so what they essentially meant was 'Dark Spielberg'.

(222)

Finn Wolfhard said he was quite touched when some Stranger Things fans made a giant quilt with Mike Wheeler's face on it.

(223)

Stranger Things 4 has the Byers family and Eleven moving to California. Netflix used their Albuquerque Studios in New Mexico studios as a base for these scenes.

(224)

Jennifer Jason Leigh as Stacy Hamilton in the 1982 film Fast Times at Ridgemont High was an influence on the clothes Nancy Wheeler wears in Stranger Things. Fast Times at Ridgemont High has been a recurring touchstone for Stranger Things. In season three, for example, Steve and Robin wear costumes similar to the pirate costumes from the Captain Hook Fish & Chip scenes in Fast Times at Ridgemont High.

(225)

In 2021, Millie Bobby Brown made a generous donation to a food bank in New Mexico while shooting Stranger Things 4.

(226)

The sequence where Eleven takes out Brenner's agents in the school corridor in the season one finale is well staged in the way that it makes the children appear very small (just as they are) and stresses their status as little underdog hobbits in this strange and bewildering battle.

Eleven must use her powers for them to have any chance of escape. A startling and fantastic sequence comes when time freezes and Eleven fixes her meanest stare in intense concentration. The Brenner squad are then 'Scannered', as a Cronenberg fan might say - minus the head explosions naturally.

(227)

The Duffers said that the finale of Stranger Things 2 was

originally going to feature a number of Easter eggs that would anticipate Stranger Things 3. However, they altered this plan and decided to remove anything that might 'box' them in when it came to writing the next season.

(228)

Finn Wolfhard said that after Stranger Things 2 came out he got asked to attend a lot of Snow Ball style school dances. He politely declined these invitations.

(229)

Gaten Matarazzo said that when Stranger Things first became available to stream on Netflix in 2016 he had a special binge watching party with his family to celebrate.

He said he was the only person though who made it through all eight episodes without falling asleep!

(230)

Millie Bobby Brown said she and Finn Wolfhard are just good friends in real life and any romance is strictly confined to their characters in Stranger Things.

(231)

According to The Hawkins Middle School Yearbook/Hawkins High School Yearbook, the ambition of Max Mayfield is to be a professional skateboarder.

(232)

Millie Bobby Brown says she always misses playing Eleven during breaks between production on Stranger Things.

(233)

The Halloween party that Steve and Nancy attend in Stranger Things 2 takes some inspiration from the 1993 film Dazed and Confused.

(234)

Finn Wolfhard said that he and Millie Bobby Brown never have any preparation or discussions for kissing scenes between Mike and Eleven in Stranger Things.

(235)

The Duffers said that Eleven was much more feral and violent in their original plans for Stranger Things. The character was toned down somewhat in the end - although she's still pretty deadly if you back her into a corner!

(236)

Stranger Things costume designer Kim Wilcox had fun during the scenes in Stranger Things 2 where Nancy and Steve go to a fancy dress party at Tina's house. The extras are dressed in all manner of movie costumes. Flashdance, Bluto from Animal House, Rocky Balboa, the Karate Kid. There is even a Madonna and Siouxsie Sioux. Look out for Glennellen Anderson's Nicole dressed as Ariel Moore from Footloose.

(237)

Millie Bobby Brown said she would like to see Mike and Eleven get married at the end of Stranger Things.

(238)

The only two of the kids in Stranger Things who never met Dr Brenner in the show are Will Byers and Max.

(239)

The X-Men comic was an influence on Eleven's story in Stranger Things - specifically The Dark Phoenix Saga. This is a comic by Chris Claremont and John Byrne that collects together X-Men #129-137. It is referenced in Stranger Things season one.

The story concerns the mutant superhero team facing a great crisis when the telekinetic Jean Grey is transformed into the all powerful Dark Phoenix.

(240)

Murray Bauman is a journalist we meet in season two. Murray has numerous conspiracy theories about Hawkins which Hopper naturally doesn't want to listen to (lest the real truth should come out). Murray eventually comes into the orbit of Jonathan and Nancy and they hatch a scheme to discredit the lab for the sake of Barb's parents. Murray is an eccentric man who lives a rather shambling existence in his apartment. He is paranoid and loves vodka but does have an engaging cynical wit.

In the pitch book for Montauk, Terry Ives is not the catatonic mother of Eleven but an eccentric male conspiracy theorist with huge spectacles who keeps pestering Hopper with paranoid warnings about suspicious secret activity at Camp Hero. The character of Terry Ives in the Montauk pitch is clearly the basis for Murray Bauman.

(241)

Millie Bobby Brown said that when she first watched Stranger Things 3 she watched a few episodes and then skipped to the finale to see how it would end.

She then went back and watched it in the correct order.

(242)

The exterior location for Hopper's woodland cabin in Stranger Things is Sleepy Hollow Farm in Powder Spring, Georgia. You can visit this farm in real life should you wish. The farm has a food store, a corn maze, and a pumpkin patch. They even sell Christmas trees.

Hopper's cabin is designed to evoke memories of the spooky forest cabin in Sam Raimi's Evil Dead films. The interiors for Hopper's cabin are shot in a studio in Atlanta.

(243)

930 Garibaldi Street Southwest, Atlanta, was used for the home of Lonnie Byers in season one. Lonnie Byers is the ex-husband of Joyce and estranged father of Will and Jonathan. Lonnie shows up in season one when Jonathan visits him to see if the missing Will might have gone to see his father.

After Will is presumed to be dead, Lonnie goes to see Joyce to lend support but we eventually learn that his main motive seems to be making a claim against the quarry where Will 'died' so that he can reap a financial windfall.

(244)

Finn Wolfhard thinks that Mike Wheeler is a trifle more serious than he is in real life.

(245)

Season two costume designer Kim Wilcox said that some of the boys grew considerably taller while shooting Stranger Things 2 and this made designing their clothes more complex.

The costume department even had to resort to a constantly updated height chart to keep track of the changes.

(246)

Eleven had 171 lines in Stranger Things 2. At the time of writing, this is the most amount of lines Eleven has had in any season of the show.

(247)

Millie Bobby Brown won the Best TV Actress award for Stranger Things at the 2017 Fangoria Chainsaw Awards.

(248)

The DVD release of season one of Stranger Things by Target was designed so that the DVD case resembled a faded old VHS tape.

(249)

Millie Bobby Brown said she would be open to appearing in an Eleven spin-off show after Stranger Things ends.

(250)

Bob Newby was only supposed to be in Stranger Things 2 for a couple of episodes. The original plan was for Bob to be killed by the Upside Down possessed Will Byers (which would have been rather dark). More than anything it was Sean Astin who altered this plan. Astin impressed the Duffers with his performance and so they ended up keeping Bob around for most of the season. The cast also loved working with Sean Astin and wanted him to stick around as long as possible.

The Duffers said that Bob Newby was more of a dope in their original plan but Sean Astin made the character more three-dimensional and rounded. Although he was a new character who we didn't get to know for long it is a tribute to Astin's performance that we feel a great sense of loss when Bob is killed by those pesky DemoDogs at the lab.

(251)

Nancy has a Debbie Harry poster in season one. Debbie Harry was the lead singer of punkish pop band Blondie and a huge star and sex symbol in the early 1980s.

(252)

Millie Bobby Brown said that even when she became world famous after the first season of Stranger Things she still had to do homework and chores when she was at home.

(253)

The decision to make Robin gay in season three was only taken after two or three episodes were already in the can.

Upon reflection, everyone felt that Robin and Steve becoming a romantic couple would be too predictable a storyline.

(254)

Camp Hero in Montauk is now part of a state park. Parts of the old military base though are still closed off to the public and guarded - which does make you wonder what they are still hiding.

You can hike or ramble through this area but you won't be allowed to explore the defunct military base which greatly inspired Stranger Things.

(255)

Eleven's happy reaction to finally seeing Mike again in the penultimate episode of Stranger Things 2 was a great piece of acting by Millie Bobby Brown because Finn Wolfhard wasn't on the set that day and Millie had to react to nothing.

(256)

Dustin has been to Camp Know Where at the start of season three of Stranger Things. Camp Nowhere is a 1994 film starring Christopher Lloyd

(257)

Dr Brenner was known simply as Agent one in the pilot script for Montauk. The Duffers said the character of Brenner was a little on the vague side until Matthew Modine came onboard. In the original treatment for Stranger Things (or Montauk as it would have been), Dr Brenner/Agent One was dressed casually in jeans and a lumberjack shirt. Matthew Modine decided to make Brenner more stuffy and unemotional.

Movie buffs think that Dr Brenner is deliberately made to look like David Cronenberg's villain in the Clive Barker film Nightbreed. Cronenberg is a famous horror movie director (in addition to being an occasional actor) and his films include The Fly, Dead Ringers, and Scanners.

Modine has suggested though that Brenner's hair is based on Robert Shaw in the war film Battle of the Bulge.

(258)

Millie Bobby Brown did her audition when the show was still called Montauk. Millie said she didn't have the faintest idea what the show was about. All she knew was that it had science fiction and was set in the 1980s.

(259)

Dustin Henderson was described as wearing spectacles in the early plans for Stranger Things but he doesn't wear glasses in the actual show.

(260)

Finn Wolfhard has played Dungeons & Dragons online with some of the other Stranger Things cast members.

(261)

At the Palace Arcade in Stranger Things 2 you can see a game called Quest for the Space Knife. This game is fictitious and based on the fact that one of the production crew had a music band called Space Knife.

(262)

Eleven's hair in season one of Stranger Things could be an unconscious Alien 3 Easter egg. Sigourney Weaver shaved her hair for the film because her character Ripley lands on a prison planet that has a big problem with lice.

(263)

One of the most obvious riffs on Indiana Jones and the Temple of Doom in Stranger Things 2 comes when Jonathan and Nancy play out a flirtatious bedroom farce at Bauman's house in the manner of Harrison Ford and Kate Capshaw in the palace scenes in the film.

(264)

The Empire Strikes back is the inspiration for the scene in The Lost Sister where Eleven tries to move the train with her powers. It mirrors Luke trying to raise the X-Wing from the swamp when he is being trained by Yoda.

(265)

Finn Wolfhard said that when he became famous through Stranger Things his family had to change their telephone number.

(266)

The scene where the DemoDogs attack Bob and Hopper drags Joyce away could be interpreted as a nod to the scene in Aliens where Vasquez is reluctantly dragged away after her friend Drake is laced with acid and about to be killed by the Xenomorphs.

(267)

The moment where Lucas shoots the Demogorgon in the season one finale with his wrist-rocket and it flies back (we quickly deduce that Eleven REALLY did this - not Lucas) is a homage to the scene in Saving Private Ryan where Tom Hanks fires a futile shot at a tank just as the tank is about to be bombed by an aircraft.

(268)

When they shot the school classroom Demogorgon showdown in the Stranger Things season one finale, the children were in a silly mood and kept laughing during takes.

(269)

The scripts on Stranger Things are quite fluid in that the Duffers like to give themselves enough flexibility to change plot points - even during production.

This is why the actors in the show never seem to be completely sure what is actually going to happen in any given season.

(270)

Finn Wolfhard said that the directors have never tried to mask his (rapidly expanding) height in Stranger Things.

(271)

When Joyce takes an axe to the wall in season one, this is a homage to Jack Nicholson in Kubrick's The Shining.

(272)

Music from the John Hughes film Pretty in Pink can be heard during the funeral of Will Byers in season one.

(273)

Shannon Purser said that when her time on Stranger Things ended she wanted to take home Barb's spectacles as a memento but - alas - she wasn't able to do this for some reason.

(274)

In terms of broad inspiration, Stranger Things 3 goes all in on both versions of Invasion of the Body Snatchers and also returns, yet again, to John Carpenter's The Thing.

(275)

Stranger Things 3 draws some obvious inspiration from Martin Brest's 1988 film Midnight Run when Hopper and Joyce hit the road with their prisoner.

You even hear some of the music from the film.

(276)

Mike Wheeler has a deliberate resemblance in season one of Stranger Things to Henry Thomas in the 1984 kids spy film Cloak & Dagger.

(277)

Finn Wolfhard said that when he went back to school after season one of Stranger Things came out he wasn't really treated any differently by the other pupils.

(278)

Steve Harrington having to wear a silly costume (which makes it much more difficult to pick up girls) in Stranger Things 3 mirrors Judge Reinhold's character having to do the same thing in Fast Times at Ridgemont High.

(279)

The colours for the Upside Down scenes in the season one finale was toned down so that the lights of the hazmat suits would be heightened.

(280)

Mind Flayers are called Illithids in Dungeons & Dragons. Illithids are fearsome humanoid aberrations with psionic powers.

(281)

The Duffers didn't have a name for Dr Owens at first so in the early Stranger Things 2 script drafts they called him Dr Paul Reiser in tribute to Carter Burke (who was obviously played by Reiser) from James Cameron's 1986 film Aliens.

(282)

Millie Bobby Brown had to play scenes with various boys who were in contention to play Mike Wheeler during the casting process. When she played a scene with Finn Wolfhard and had excellent chemistry with him the casting department knew they had found their Mike Wheeler.

(283)

The slug coughed up by Will Byers at the end of the season one finale was made of candy and apple sauce.

(284)

Shannon Purser first started attending auditions at the age of 15. She got the acting bug through school plays and community theater.

(285)

One would think that Invasion of the Body Snatchers - a big influence on Stranger Things 3 - would neatly fit into the Red Scare theme but this is not the case.

The 1956 version is alleged to be laced with a multitude of apparent hidden meanings on everything from the Communist Witchhunts to the FBI and yet the author of the original novel and the director of the film always maintained that no grand political metaphor was intended and it was primarily just a science fiction story about aliens from outer space taking over human beings.

(286)

There are a number of food anachronisms in season one. Eleven eats Pringles from a 1960s tub, Dustin has a Pez dispenser from 1999, and when Eleven steals waffles from the supermarket you can see brands of modern chewing gum by the cash registers.

(287)

The sexism of the men at the Hawkins newspaper office in Stranger Things 3 was loosely inspired by the 1980 Dolly Parton film 9 to 5.

(288)

The relationship between Dustin and Erica is surprisingly rewarding through the course of Stranger Things 3 in the way that Dustin gradually makes Erica question her own apparent disdain for nerds. By the end of the season Erica will look at nerds in a new light. She will discover that - horror of horrors - she might even be a nerd herself.

(289)

The production budget for the development of the original Dungeons & Dragons board game was only $2,000. A mere $100 of that was allocated to the artwork.

(290)

Bob deciding to watch the movie Mr Mom at Halloween is a meta joke because Winona Ryder got an early break acting with Mr Mom star Michael Keaton in Tim Burton's Beetlejuice.

Bob wearing a Dracula costume at Halloween is another joke as Winona starred in Francis Ford Coppola's version of Dracula in the early nineties.

(291)

Erica's vent crawling in season three is very Die Hard but also reminds one of the android Bishop in Aliens crawling through conduits to the transmitter so he can remotely pilot the Sulaco's remaining dropship.

(292)

Dean Zimmerman, the Stranger Things editor, said that of the two twins who played Holly Wheeeler in season one, one of them was definitely better than the other when it came to reactions and acting.

(293)

Eleven's makeover in The Lost Sister makes her look somewhat like Ally Sheedy in The Breakfast Club.

(294)

Stranger Things 3 almost entirely eschews sequences set in the Upside Down. It feels like a conscious attempt to give Stranger Things 3 a fresh personality as far as one can in the somewhat constrictive universe of the show.

(295)

Matt Duffer said he finds alternate dimensions and aliens scarier than ghosts because there is more chance that they actually exist.

(296)

It is estimated that over four billion minutes of Dungeons and Dragons content has been viewed on Twitch.

(297)

David Harbour said it was a rather surreal experience to see his likeness on Stranger Things toys and action figures.

(298)

The Duffer Brothers said they would turn down an offer to direct a big Hollywood movie while Stranger Things is still in production because they can only concentrate on one thing at a time.

(299)

There have been a number of Stranger Things comics but so far they've been rather disappointing. One of the problems with the Stranger Things comics is that they are clearly at pains not to tread on the toes of the television show so tend to be side stories or prequels. Some of them even take place between seasons of the show. The plots of the comics include previous tales of children at Brenner's lab, the kids making a home movie at Halloween, Dustin away at science camp, Hopper sneaking Eleven out to Christmas dinner at the Byers house, and also a comic all about those odious season one school bullies Troy and James.

The best Stranger Things comic is still probably the first one (by Jody Hauser) - which basically shows us what happened to Will Byers while he was trapped in the Upside Down. Even this comic is no great shakes but it's better than what came after. The Stranger Things comics tend mostly to be aimed at younger children (which obviously means that the horror and language is very mild) and the art is nothing to write home about. We may have to wait until the television show has actually ended to get a really great Stranger Things comic.

(300)

The Duffers said that the use of MKUltra in Stranger Things was essentially a plot device through which they could infuse the show with science based horror.

(301)

In season one of Stranger Things there was a determination to, as far as possible, use practical effects rather than CGI. In some cases though this proved impossible. To give an example, the Duffers said that when they tried to do a sequence where the Demogorgon smashes through a wall it looked ridiculous when they did it in a practical way so they had to resort to computer generated effects.

(302)

The Hawkins Department of Energy building in Stranger

Things is really the former Georgia Mental Health Institute.

The Georgia Mental Health Institute (GMHI) was a psychiatric hospital which operated from 1965 to 1997 near Emory University in Druid Hills near Atlanta Georgia. The site was later purchased by Emory University from the state of Georgia.

(303)

The original cut of Bob Newby's death in Stranger Things 2 was more gruesome and blood splattered. The Duffer Brothers said they toned his death down somewhat because they thought the blood and gore was a trifle on the gratuitous side.

Sean Astin was very happy with the death scene because he'd wanted Bob to have a heroic and memorable demise in the show.

(304)

David Harbour officiated a wedding in 2018 in his Hawkins police uniform. His only condition on agreeing to do this was that he got the first slice of wedding cake.

The couple who got married were obviously big Stranger Things fans.

(305)

The filming location for the Hawkins Post in season three is 6981 Main Street Lithonia, GA.

(306)

Shooting the scene in the season two finale where Eleven closes the gate to the Upside down made Millie Bobby Brown nauseous because she was on a platform that had a swaying motion.

(307)

The main reason the Duffers wanted an electronic score in Stranger Things was to mitigate the overtly Spielbergian DNA of the show.

(308)

The pilot script for Montauk features strange electrical storms. In the actual show this element was only introduced in season two.

(309)

According to The Hawkins Middle School Yearbook/Hawkins High School Yearbook, Steve Harrington is undecided about what occupation he wants to go into when he is older.

(310)

The Duffer Brothers say that they like to binge television shows rather than watch them once a week. Stranger Things is very much designed for the 'bingers' among us.

(311)

Noah Schnapp was the smallest of the boys in season one. By season four however he was the second tallest after Finn Wolfhard.

(312)

The Duffer Brothers said it was shows like True Detective and The Knick that made them excited about working in television (or streaming as the case may be).

They said they love the long form nature of television.

(313)

The Duffer Brothers feel that if they had pitched Stranger Things as a movie it probably wouldn't been produced by anyone.

They didn't really have any clout in Hollywood at the time.

(314)

Millie Bobby Brown said she was sad when she saw that Mike and Eleven were going to break up in season three.

(315)

When Eleven hurls the car (mentally of course) at the baddies in the mall in season three this car stunt was practical and not a digital special effect.

(316)

A season four episode is titled Vecna's Curse. Vecna was a wizard in Dungeons & Dragons. The character is known as the God of Secrets.

(317)

Eleven at school in Stranger Things 4 clearly draws some inspiration from Stephen King's Carrie. Carrie White struggled to fit in at school too.

(318)

Nancy Wheeler is a character in Judy Blume's cultish young fiction novel Are You There God? It's Me, Margaret.

This connection is purely accidental by all accounts.

(319)

In the gap between the first two seasons, David Harbour said that if season one of Stranger Things was a delicious vanilla ice cream then Stranger Things 2 would have to be a delicious strawberry ice cream. His point was that you couldn't just give everyone vanilla ice cream all over again. Strangely though, people sometimes say that season two was just a rehash of season one - which feels unfair because Stranger Things 2 is plainly trying to give you something different.

It separates Eleven from the children, teams up Eleven and Hopper, has an episode set in a city, introduces the Mind Flayer, teams up Steve and Dustin, has a new head of the laboratory, and introduces new characters in Max, Bob, Billy, Kali, and Murray.

(320)

Dacre Montgomery caught the eye in his Stranger Things audition tape by dancing to Duran Duran's Hungry Like the Wolf.

(321)

Hasbro released a retro handheld Stranger Things game where you could play twenty vintage arcade games like Galaxian and Pac-Man.

(322)

Jonathan Byers says in season one that his brother Will is very good at hiding. This is as good an explanation as any for why Will was able to survive in the Upside Down.

(323)

The young Broadway star Eli Tokash said that he sent in a taped audition for Stranger Things/Montauk (presumably he was hoping to play one of the boys in the show) but never heard back from anyone.

(324)

Dacre Montgomery came up with the moment in Will the Wise where Billy grabs Max by the wrist. Dacre Montgomery and Sadie Sink worked on this moment together before the scene was shot so that it would be safe.

(325)

Finn Wolhard thinks that the Demogorgon is less scary than Pennywise the Clown.

(326)

Joyce Byers going crazy through her insistence that Will is alive in season one was inspired by Richard Dreyfuss in Close Encounters of the Third kind (the Dreyfuss character becomes increasingly eccentric after he witnesses a UFO).

(327)

That's a cardboard cut-out of Phoebe Cates from Fast Times at Ridgemont High that Steve bumps into in the video store at the end of season three.

(328)

There are some obvious references to the film Predator in Stranger Things. Hopper is the name of the Green Beret that the team find dead in the 1987 film and Hawkins is also the name of a character played by Shane Black in the movie.

(329)

Elle (El) is a character in Silent Hill: Homecoming. The Last of Us, a 2013 video game about a journey across a post-apocalyptic United States, features a girl named Ellie. This is another possible source for Eleven's name in Stranger Things.

(330)

Deputy Powell is one of Hopper's deputies. He has quite a dry-wit - especially when on duty with the slightly bumbling Callahan. Powell is the name of a character in the original Die Hard film.

(331)

In reality the Department of Energy (DOE) is a Cabinet-level department of the United States Government concerned with the United States' policies regarding energy and safety in handling nuclear material.

Its duties include the nuclear weapons program, nuclear reactor production for the United States Navy, energy conservation, energy-related research, radioactive waste disposal, and domestic energy production.

(332)

Millie Bobby Brown did some method acting for the scene at the end of season three when Eleven reads Hopper's letter from beyond the grave. Millie only read the dialogue in Hopper's letter for the first time when she did the scene.

(333)

The original edition of Dungeons & Dragons initially produced about a thousand copies. These sold out in weeks and set the game on the path to becoming hugely famous.

(334)

The filming location for the abandoned Brimborn Steel Works in season three was 2903 RN Martin Street East Point, GA.

(335)

In preparation for shooting on season one, some stores in Jackson had to be modified to make them look as if they were from 1983. The Radio Shack store's front was stocked with period accurate items which included black and white televisions and an Atari.

(336)

According to The Hawkins Middle School Yearbook/Hawkins High School Yearbook, the ambition of Lucas Sinclair is to be a police detective.

(337)

In Dungeons & Dragons, thessalmonsters are a group of related creatures designed to resemble the hydra. The thessalhydra first appeared in first edition in the original Monster Manual II. The creature features in the boys' Dungeons & Dragons game in episode eight. This anticipates the hydra-like Mind Flayer in season two.

(338)

Shannon Purser said she ended up with a few bruises after shooting Barb's violent struggle with the Demogorgon at the Harrington pool.

(339)

Kyle Lambert created the famous Stranger Things posters. His brief was to mimic the hand painted film posters of the 1980s.

(340)

Joe Chrest plays the permanently oblivious Ted Wheeler in Stranger Things. Chrest has appeared in everything from Columbo to Deadwood. He is also a music professor.

(341)

Matt Duffer said the apparent death of Brenner in season one was purposely ambiguous.

(342)

The music in Stranger Things is heavily influenced by Tangerine Dream. Tangerine Dream is a German electronic music band formed in 1967 by Edgar Froese. They have composed many movie scores - including Legend, Near Dark, The Keep, Firestarter, and Risky Business.

Stranger Things used three Tangerine Dream tracks in its soundtrack: "Green Desert" from Green Desert (1986), "Exit" from Exit (1981) and "Tangent (Rare Bird)" from Poland (1984).

The mutual appreciation society runs deep as Tangerine Dream starting including their own version of the Stranger Things theme in their live sets.

(343)

David Harbour said that out of the kids in Stranger Things he related to Mike Wheeler the most. The Duffers said the same thing.

(344)

Netflix agreed to produce Stranger Things before they'd even seen a single script. They agreed to make the show based purely on the concept and the pitch material the Duffers had provided.

(345)

The very first Dungeons & Dragons monster manual referred to the Demogorgon as Lord Of All That Swims In Darkness.

(346)

The ramshackle trailer that Hopper lives in during season one was purchased by the Stranger Things art department for $1.

(347)

The success of Stranger Things has been very important to Netflix because it has essentially given the platform their first franchise. Stranger Things had little merch or promotion in its first season but now Stranger Things merch is all over the place and there have been video games, commercial deals with brands like Cocoa-Cola and Nike, and even talk of Stranger Things spin-off shows when the series ends.

It seems inevitable that Netflix will not want the Stranger Things brand to lay dormant when the show ends and be looking for ways to bring it back in some form or other. We have seen this with big movie franchises like Star Wars and even Harry Potter.

(348)

Netflix picked up nearly seven million extra subscribers in the third quarter of 2019.

The majority of these new subscriptions were attributed to the release of Stranger Things 3.

(349)

In Dungeons & Dragons, Lucas was a Knight in season one but a Ranger in season two.

(350)

Matthew Modine said that Brenner's shoes were inspired by a pair that President Kennedy used to wear.

(351)

Gaten Matarazzo says that when he finishes shooting a season on Stranger Things the first thing he does is get his hair cut because he finds Dustin's long hair to be a pain in real life. Gaten tends to wear his hair shorter in real life than Dustin Henderson does in Stranger Things.

(352)

Finn Wolfhard said of the contrast between his characters in Stranger Things and Stephen King's IT that Richie is super annoying while Mike is more of a leader.

(353)

The rather iconic dress that Eleven wears in season one is based on the Polly Flinders brand of dresses (which were popular in the 1970s). The embroidery on the dress was done by hand by the costume department.

This dress (worn with Mike's blue jacket) was a popular Halloween costume in 2016.

(354)

When Billy is in his car and threatens to run the boys over in season two he asks Max if he'll get earn 'points' for hitting them all at once. This is a reference to the 1975 movie Death Race 2000. In that film a dystopian future has a violent car race where you get points for running over pedestrians.

(355)

Maya Hawke had to do some audition scenes with Joe Keery before she was cast as Robin Buckley in Stranger Things 3. The producers obviously wanted to make sure that Steve and Robin would have good chemistry in the show.

Maya is the daughter of the famous actors Uma Thurman and Ethan Hawke. She was very nervous about appearing in Stranger Things 3.

Maya said she turned her social media off the day it became available to stream in case of any criticism. She needn't have worried though because Robin proved to be a very popular new character.

(356)

The children in the Stranger Things cast were given tutors and their own classroom on the set of the first couple of seasons.

Despite their growing fame they still had to continue their education.

(357)

In The Mall Rats episode, 765 is suggested as the area code for Indiana. At the time though the code was 317.

(358)

The Lost Sister uses a piece of music from a deleted scene in John Carpenter's Escape from New York.

(359)

Matthew Modine as Dr Brenner has about forty lines in season one.

(360)

Finn Wolfhard said that Mike Wheeler will always be the part dearest to his heart because it was his big break and launched his career.

(361)

The first episode of season four (The Hellfire Club) is the first season debut episode not to have the name of a character in its title.

(362)

David Harbour chipped a tooth shooting the tunnel sequences in Stranger Things 2. Harbour also had to do a dangerous stunt when Eleven shatters the windows in the cabin. That's really David Harbour standing there because a dummy or stunt double would have been too obvious.

(363)

Shawn Levy said that on season one he was very impressed that Millie Bobby Brown would ask permission to do another take for a scene if she felt she could improve it even more.

Despite her youth, she was clearly very dedicated and enthusiastic when it came to her craft.

(364)

The primary typeface for Stranger Things art and its titles is Benguiat. This typeface is heavily associated with Stephen King paperbacks from the 1980s.

(365)

Eduardo Franco plays pizza delivery driver Argyle in Stranger Things 4. Argyle is the name of the limo driver in the original Die Hard.

(366)

The younger version of Billy Hargrove in E Pluribus Unum was portrayed by Christopher Convery. Convery is a child actor who has appeared in shows that include Gotham and MacGyver.

(367)

The costume department on season one said they came up with a preppy look for Steve Harrington. Preppy means of or typical of a pupil or graduate of an expensive prep school, especially with reference to their neat style of dress.

Steve doesn't go to an exclusive school but we can clearly see that his family is quite rich because they have a swimming pool and Steve drives a BMW.

(368)

Sarah Hindsgaul, the hairstylist on Stranger Things, said that Steve's preposterously elaborate quiff in season one was designed to make him visually annoying.

(369)

Gaten Matarazzo formed something of a double act with Caleb McLaughlin in the very early promotional tours for Stranger Things. They did a lot of interviews together.

(370)

Dean Zimmerman, the Stranger Things editor, said he was surprised to see Benny killed off so quickly in the first episode. Zimmerman presumed that an actor of Chris Sullivan's calibre would get a more recurring or meatier part.

(371)

In the pilot script for Montauk, Benny's Burgers is called Benny's Fish 'n Fry. When Eleven sneaks into the diner she bites into a cod that she finds in the freezer.

(372)

The scene where Lucas uses fireworks to distract the monster in the mall was one of the most complex and difficult scenes to shoot in Stranger Things 3. Trivia - it wasn't actually legal to buy fireworks in Indiana in 1985.

(373)

Hopper has a Smith and Wesson Model 66 firearm in the first season. In the second season he has a Colt Python.

(374)

The dance in the John Hughes film 16 Candles was a big influence on the design of the Snow Ball in the season two finale.

(375)

The Montauk pilot script has a goof because it implies Dustin owns a copy of Uncanny X-Men 269. However, this comic only came out in 1990 and the pilot script takes place in 1980.

(376)

Millie Bobby Brown's hair grew considerably by the time season two began shooting. For the scene at the start of Trick or Treat, Freak, a flashback has Eleven trapped in the Upside Down version of the school in the immediate moments after the school classroom showdown in the finale. To convey Eleven's buzzcut from season one, they had to put a bald cap on Millie Bobby Brown and then CGI her short hair in.

(377)

David Harbour said that when he was shooting the first season of Stranger Things he had no idea if anyone would actually watch the show when it came out.

(378)

Stranger Things is not terribly consistent when it comes to the name of Hopper's late daughter. In captions she is Sarah but in scripts she is Sara.

(379)

In the pilot script for Montauk, Joyce Byers is a Long Island waitress who swears a lot.

(380)

Karen Wheeler was described as having blonde hair in the Montauk pilot script. This wasn't the case in Stranger Things - though Karen goes quite blonde in season three.

(381)

The original plan was for Eleven to be completely bald in season one but the hairdressing department felt this would make the character look too aggressive.

(382)

The Duffer Brothers said they cast the kids in Stranger Things as early as possible so they would have time to tailor the scripts and characters to the personalities of the children.

(383)

The Upside Down in Stranger Things owes something to Planet of the Vampires. Planet of the Vampires (Terrore nello spazio) is a cult 1965 pulp gothic horror space opera by Italian maestro Mario Bava. If you want to know where the main inspiration for Ridley Scott's Alien came from then look no further than Planet of the Vampires. In the film twin starships Galliott and Argos are in uncharted space when they receive a distress signal from an unexplored world named Aura.

violence. Aura is an unsettling nightmare world of dense billowing fog, desolate rocks and strange eerie pulsating lights.

(384)

David Harbour said that Hopper's early arc in Stranger Things 4 is influenced by Alien 3 and The Great Escape.

(385)

There is a telephone number mentioned in Stranger Things 3 when Hopper is on the line with an operator. The number is 618-625-8313. Those that called this number in real life got a special message delivered by Brett Gelman as Murray Bauman.

(386)

In a very early plan for Stranger Things, Lonnie Byers was going to return in the finale and help Jonathan and Nancy fight the Demogorgon. This was changed when Steve Harrington was allocated a bigger part and a redemptive character arc. As we now know, it is Steve and not Lonnie who assists Jonathan and Nancy in battling the Demogorgon in the season one finale.

(387)

When the first images of season two were released, some entertainment sites said Millie Bobby Brown had been given an eighties perm as Eleven. That wasn't true at all. Eleven's curly hair in season two is Millie Bobby Brown's real natural hair.

(388)

Shawn Levy has a cameo in the season one episode The Body as a morgue worker.

(389)

Dustin believes Dart might be the Indirana semipalmata species of frog in season two. This genus of frog wasn't classified until 1986 though.

(390)

The fights between Hopper and Grigori in Stranger Things 3 took some inspiration from the fight between Indiana Jones and Pat Roach's hulking German soldier at the airfield in Raiders of the Lost Ark.

(391)

The Stranger Things YouTube channel receives about ten million views a month.

(392)

The Stranger Things opening title sequence is constructed to look like a cryptic puzzle that is slowly revealing itself.

(393)

According to The Hawkins Middle School Yearbook/Hawkins High School Yearbook, the ambition of Dustin Henderson is to be a Cryptozoologist. This is the study of unclassified creatures.

(394)

The song "Go Nowhere" by the band Reagan Youth is briefly heard on a car radio in season one. This is a mistake because the song only came out in 1984 and season one is set in 1983.

(395)

Dustin sports a Casio F-91W digital watch in Stranger Things

2. These watches only came out in 1991.

(396)

When he was directing The Spy, Andrew Stanton set up a shot involving Joyce Byers to mimic a shot of Peter Finch in the 1976 film Network.

(397)

The Duffer Brothers said that their original plan for Stranger Things was much darker but it became somewhat lighter after they cast the kids.

(398)

Steve Harrington's hair in season two was heavily influenced by singer Morten Harket in the 1980s Norwegian pop band A-ha.

(399)

Stranger Things 2 began production with a secret codename because the media and fans were so rabid for spoilers after the amazing success of season one.

(400)

The apparent death of Hopper in Stranger Things 3 was a suggestion by David Harbour.

(401)

Kali's gang in season two are loosely inspired by the gang in the 1979 Walter Hill film The Warriors.

(402)

Netflix were so impressed with the footage they saw during the production of season one that they gave the Duffers a bigger budget for the finale.

(403)

Will and Dustin both have Ghostbusters lunchboxes at school in season two.

(404)

Finn Wolfhard said it was somewhat overwhelming when the first season of Stranger Things became such a phenomenon. A few times some autograph hunters followed him home - which he found quite alarming.

(405)

Robin says a line in Stranger Things 3 that is almost identical to a line in the 1992 Robert Redford film Sneakers.

(406)

The Duffer Brothers said that 99% of child actors would not have been capable of fronting a big dramatic show in the way that Millie, Finn, Gaten, Caleb, and Noah did in season one.

(407)

Gaten Matarazzo thinks he can do a good impression of Millie Bobby Brown's English accent!

(408)

The monster clawing through the wall in season one is a reference to a similar scene in A Nightmare On Elm Street.

(409)

A flyer protesting against the mall in Stranger Things 3 is

based on the save the clocktower flyer from Back to the Future.

(410)

The Duffer Brothers have a secret thirty page document which lays out the basic rules of the Upside Down. They did this so that the depiction of the Upside Down would be fairly consistent.

(411)

In 1973, then-CIA-director Richard Helms ordered all documents relating to MKUltra destroyed. However, 20,000 pages of documents survived because of a filing error.

This is how the secret of the MKUltra experiments came to light.

(412)

Billy calls a kid 'lard ass' at the pool in season three in reference to the pie-eating contest in Stand By Me.

(413)

Joe Keery was born in Newburyport, Massachusetts and attended River Valley Charter School for elementary and middle school, and then Newburyport High School. He later studied at The Theatre School at DePaul University. His first roles came in commercials, including one for KFC - which might qualify the scene in Stranger Things 2 where Steve eats KFC with Barb's parents as an in-joke!

(414)

Matt Duffer said that the scene in Stranger Things 2 where Will Byers screams as the kids burn the Upside Down took twenty hours to edit.

(415)

The Hellfire Club, the title of an episode in season four, is the name of a secret society in the X-Men comics. It plays a key role in the Dark Phoenix storyline - which was one of but many inspirations for Eleven. The origin of the name Hellfire Club comes from exclusive gentleman's clubs for high society hellraisers in 18th century England. In season four of Stranger Things, the Hellfire Club refers to a group that plays Dungeons & Dragons.

(416)

Millie Bobby Brown said that the kids on Stranger Things are always stealing one another's potato chips on the set.

(417)

Sadie Sink was born in Brenham, Texas. An obsession with Disney's High School Musical led her to take acting classes in community theatre and at the age of eleven a Broadway audition landed her a role in the revival of Annie. Her television roles include Blue Bloods and The Americans and she featured in eleven episodes of the thriller series American Odyssey.

Sadie had a small role in the 2016 film Chuck, which starred Liev Schreiber and told the story of boxer Chuck Wepner. She also appeared in the 2017 film The Glass Castle, which starred Brie Larson and Woody Harrelson.

(418)

The Stranger Things editor Dean Zimmerman said when they were shooting episode seven of season one they shot an extra scene to put in episode one (The Vanishing of Will Byers). He didn't seem to say which scene this was. The elevator prologue maybe?

(419)

Gaten Matarazzo and Joe Keery seemed to match their looks at the 2018 Sage Awards. They both had slicked back hair and black outfits.

(420)

The film that Steve smuggles the kids in to watch at the mall at the start of season three is Day of the Dead. Day of the Dead is the last film in George Romero's classic original zombie trilogy.

Day of the Dead is set in an underground army missile bunker near the Florida Everglades (a 25-acre limestone mine in Pennsylvania was used for the shoot). A small group of scientists and soldiers are trapped there in an uneasy and fractious alliance - their dwindling numbers depleted by death and their despairing sense of isolation compounded by the fact that they can't contact anyone on the radio now, not even Washington. Dr Logan (Richard Liberty) speculates that the dead now outnumber the living by 400,000 to 1.

In an ironic reversal of their traditional roles, the living are underground while the dead wander around on the surface, now the masters of what used to be civilisation.

Day of the Dead is enriched by its doom laden atmosphere and builds to an enjoyably blood drenched finale.

(421)

Netflix dubbed Stranger Things into nine languages and subtitled it in twenty-two.

(422)

The scene at the end of The Mind Flayer in Stranger Things 2 when Eleven dramatically returns is a partial riff on the scene in Alien: Resurrection where Winona Ryder's android character Call is suddenly revealed again - despite apparently just dying.

(423)

Dustin's girlfriend Suzie is reading Ursula K. Le Guin's novel A Wizard Of Earthsea when we first see her in Stranger Things 3.

(424)

Gaten Matarazzo said he has one of the easiest acting jobs among the cast because he feels as if he is essentially just playing himself most of the time as Dustin.

(425)

Dart in Stranger Things 2 was voiced by the sound designer Craig Henighan.

(426)

One of the most far out fan theories is the suggestion that the Demogorgon is Will Byers from the future.

(427)

Brett Gelman as Murray was promoted to main cast regular for Stranger Things 4.

(428)

Gaten Matarazzo says that on Stranger Things the cast never get to see any scripts until they arrive in Atlanta to commence shooting.

(429)

Millie Bobby Brown as Eleven has only been absent from one

episode (The Spy) of Stranger Things.

(430)

The Duffer Brothers said that Eleven was simply a tabula rasa in their scripts and notes and that it was Millie Bobby Brown who gave the character heart and an endearing quality.

(431)

Jonathan has a poster in his room in season one which combines David Bowie's Ziggy Stardust and the 19th century French poet Arthur Rimbaud.

(432)

Stranger Things has some similarities to the Stephen King story From a Buick 8. From a Buick 8 concerns strange lights and creatures and plants that seem to belong to another dimension.

(433)

A news report of Hopper's death in the season three finale says that he was a decorated Vietnam veteran.

(434)

The Duffer Brothers had a stipulation that there shouldn't be any strings in the score on season one. They wanted an electronic score rather than an orchestral score.

One exception to this came when Peter Gabriel's cover of Heroes is heard during the scenes where Will's 'body' is found in the quarry. It was Shawn Levy who suggested that song and the Duffers evidently agreed to include it.

(435)

Matt Duffer said that Dan Simmons' 1991 novel Summer of Night was an influence on Stranger Things. Summer of Night is set in a small Illinois town in 1960 and features a gang of boys who are around twelve years-old. They must battle an evil in their small town.

(436)

Sarah Hindsgaul, the hairstylist on Stranger Things, said that Joyce Byers has deliberately terrible and unflattering hairstyles because Winona Ryder was absolutely determined that the character should look nothing like she does in real life.

(437)

The hairdressing department tried around 250 different wigs before they chose the blonde wig that Eleven wears in season one when the boys sneak her into the school.

(438)

In season one, Steve Harrington wears the same Nike shoes that Tom Cruise wore in the film All the Right Moves.

(439)

Billy Hargrove is the only character who has not been killed in the same season in which he was introduced. We met Billy in season two but he only shuffled off this mortal coil in season three.

(440)

The Duffers think that The Bathtub is the most fun episode in season one because this is the episode in which the three distinct teams (adults, teens, kids) investigating the strange goings on in Hawkins finally all coalesce and meet up.

(441)

An episode in season four is titled The Nina Project. This is assumed to be a reference to a woman named Nina Kulagina. Nina Kulagina served in the Red Army during the war and claimed to have psychic powers. She took part in many experiments in the Soviet Union in order to prove that her powers were real. Sceptics in the west though believe that she was a fraud and her powers were merely tricks and sleight of hand.

(442)

As the Hawkins lab was closed down in Stranger Things 2, there was not much need for Paul Reiser's Dr Owens in Stranger Things 3 - although he does make a very brief cameo in the finale.

(443)

Gaten Matarazzo said he has been impressed by some of the Stranger Things fan fiction he has encountered.

(444)

Kyle Dixon and Michael Stein say that although their music for Stranger Things is very retro synth at times they do seek to make the score feel modern. They have stated that if they did a completely eighties style score for Stranger Things it would probably feel a bit hokey and cheesy.

(445)

Eerie, Indiana was a television series that ran on NBC from 1991 to 1992. The mystery series for kids revolves around Marshall Teller, a teenager who moves to the strange town of Eerie, Indiana. Eerie, Indiana had a spin-off show named Eerie, Indiana: The Other Dimension which revolved around an inter-dimensional rift.

Despite all of these apparent similarities, the Duffers have said that Eerie, Indiana was not an influence on Stranger Things nor their decision to set the show in Indiana.

(446)

A number of Dustin Henderson lookalikes were enlisted to promote season two of Stranger Things at Comic Con.

(447)

The cast in Stranger Things were not given all of the scripts for season one and had no idea how the story was going to end. They were only given a fresh script for the episode they were about to shoot.

(448)

Priah Ferguson as Erica got a much bigger part in season three because she made the Duffers laugh in season two. Priah only had a few scenes in season two but she made the most of them.

(449)

Stranger Things 3 was notable in that Eleven's backstory at the lab and Dr Brenner did not feature at all. Stranger Things 4 has the return of these elements.

(450)

David Harbour shaved his head for Stranger Things 4 to avoid any resemblance with his character from Black Widow - who also spends time in a Russian prison.

(451)

When the protesters are outside city hall in season three, you can see one placard complaining about pretzels.

(452)

The man who has his car stolen by Hopper at the gas station in Stranger Things 3 is called 'Rich Douchebag Todd' in the end credits.

(453)

Millie Bobby Brown said that her lucky number in real life is not eleven but eight.

(454)

The real shooting location for Hawkins Police Station in Stranger Things is 48 Pray Street in Douglasville, Georgia.

This is the old City building right off Church Street.

(455)

A man named Mr McCorkle is mentioned in Stranger Things 2. Mr McCorkle was a neighbour of the Duffers in North Carolina when they were kids.

(456)

Gaten Matarazzo says that he shares Dustin Henderson's great love of chocolate pudding.

(457)

In Christopher Marlowe's Doctor Faustus, penned around 1590, the title character mentions the name Demogorgon while calling upon the demon Mephistopheles.

(458)

Benny Hammond, the diner owner who is killed by Connie Frazier in the first episode of Stranger Things, was named

Benny Henderson in the pilot script for Montauk. Presumably then, he was supposed to be related to Dustin in the early plans.

(459)

The hospital logos and uniforms in Stranger Things 3 are deliberately similar to the hospital logos and uniforms in the 1981 horror sequel Halloween II.

Halloween II picks up right where the original Halloween ends. Laurie Strode (Jamie Lee Curtis) is rushed to hospital as Michael Myers is on the loose again in Haddonfield after somehow surviving being shot by Dr Loomis (Donald Pleasance) and falling off the balcony. Michael eventually realises Laurie is at the hospital and goes there, killing most of the staff in the process. As ever though, Dr Loomis is on the bogeyman's trail.

(460)

Bellwood Quarry was used for the quarry scenes in season one of Stranger Things. This quarry was also used in the film The Hunger Games - Mockingjay Part 1.

(461)

Millie Bobby Brown had never seen a record player before until she visited the Stranger Things sets for the first time. This was not the case with Finn Wolfhard though. His parents had always owned a record player and vinyl albums.

(462)

According to The Hawkins Middle School Yearbook/Hawkins High School Yearbook, the ambition of Mike Wheeler is to be a writer.

(463)

Finn Wolfhard said that he first decided he wanted to become an actor after watching the Tobey Maguire Spider-Man movies.

(464)

Music score from the cult 1988 film Killer Klowns from Outer Space can be heard when Dustin's toys come to life in the first episode of season three.

(465)

In the famous scene in season one when Eleven takes the Eggos from the supermarket you can see a few cars go past outside that are way too modern for 1983.

(466)

Some of those who work on Stranger Things have said that occasionally they've had a moment where they weren't completely sure which one of the Duffer twins they were talking to. They do look pretty similar with their matching beards!

(467)

At the Halloween party in season two, Nancy and Steve are dressed as Tom Cruise and Rebecca De Mornay in the 1983 teen comedy film Risky Business.

(468)

Ray Carrol, the lab employee targeted by Kali in season two, is watching Punky Brewster on television. Punky Brewster was a sitcom aimed at younger viewers about a young girl being raised by a foster father. The show began in 1984.

(469)

David Harbour says that he's nothing like Hopper in real life. David says he's more like the boys in Stranger Things because he's a bit nerdy.

(470)

Steve's Scoops Ahoy sailor suit from season three was one of the most googled Halloween costumes in 2019. Is a sailor suit really a Halloween costume?

(471)

Dustin's elaborate bequiffed hairstyle at the Snow Ball dance comes from Jon Cryer in the John Hughes film Pretty in Pink.

(472)

The clothes that Eleven rejects during the mall montage of Eleven and Max together at the mall in season three were the actual clothes that costume designer Amy Parris and Millie Bobby Brown rejected when they were testing clothes for Eleven to wear in season three.

(473)

Kyle Dixon and Michael Stein say that composing the Stranger Things music is a surprisingly relaxed and pressure free sort of job because they have ample time to turn in their score. They said that if Stranger Things was a more conventional show which dropped new episodes on a yearly basis that definitely wouldn't be the case though.

(474)

Sean Astin as Bob Newby has about 140 lines in season two. This ranks Bob in twelfth place in that season when it comes to characters with the most lines.

(475)

Cara Buono as Karen Wheeler has 111 lines in season one. She would have less than half that amount of lines in each of the next two seasons.

(476)

The Duffers talked about wanting to put Hopper and Eleven together before season two went into production and - when filming did begin - it was noticeable that David Harbour and Millie Bobby Brown appeared at some conventions together and seemed to tease (well, Harbour did) that a father/daughter bond could be on the cards for their characters.

As a consequence, it was no surprise at all to see that Hopper was looking after Eleven in season two.

(477)

The use of mundane and seemingly placid suburbia in Stranger Things is also a feature of classic horror films like Halloween, Poltergeist, and A Nightmare On Elm Street.

(478)

A 1986 film called The Manhattan Project features a teenager who attempts to expose the nuclear secrets of a lab that is disguised as a medical company.

This film is not very well known but it does share a number of similarities to Stranger Things.

(479)

The shot of Will Byers looking into the bathroom mirror at the end of the season one finale, after he deduces that the Upside Down is not finished with him yet, is designed as a homage to the scene at the end of the original run of Twin Peaks when Agent Cooper looks into the mirror and we see that he has been infected with evil.

(480)

Max uses the word zoomer in season two. This is a modern term for Generation X. It is not an anachronism in Stranger Things though because Max is presumably making reference to liking fast things.

(481)

When Stranger Things 2 was due for release, a man named Henry Moore devised a contract with his girlfriend in which they agreed not to watch any episodes alone so that it would be impossible for either of them to reveal any spoilers.

(482)

Ted Wheeler is trying to tune his TV in to watch Knight Rider in season one. Knight Rider starred David Hasselhoff as a mysterious crime fighter with a futuristic car that had artificial intelligence.

(483)

Erica plays with one of the He-Man toys belonging to Lucas in season two. He-Man and the Masters of the Universe was a kids cartoon that ran from 1983 to 1985.

The cartoon takes place on the planet of Eternia, a planet of magic of myth. Its lead character is Prince Adam, the young son of Eternia's rulers, King Randor and Queen Marlena. Whenever Prince Adam holds the Sword of Power aloft and proclaims "By the Power of Grayskull!" he is endowed with secret powers and transformed into He-Man, the most powerful man in the universe.

(484)

Hopper reads Anne of Green Gables to Eleven in season two. He also read this book to his late daughter Sarah. Anne of Green Gables is 1908 novel by Canadian author Lucy Maud Montgomery (published as L. M. Montgomery). The book is about an orphan girl.

(485)

Maxine Mayfield has a Madrid Skateboard. This is the same brand that Marty McFly has in Back to the Future. Sadie had to do some skateboarding training in preparation for her part as Max. Because the character of Max is supposed to be from California, Sadie also had to have a little bit of fake-tan applied to make it look as if she'd recently got plenty of sun.

Sadie Sink said that one aspect of her character she doesn't share in real-life is an aptitude for video games. Max is something of an arcade fiend but Sadie said she was hopeless at the games she played in the Palace Arcade set.

(486)

When the camera tilts upside down at the end of season two you appear to see some vintage 1950s style cars almost as if Hawkins has gone back in time. The meaning of this (for it was surely intentional) has yet to be explained.

(487)

Gaten Matarazzo said the first script he got for Stranger Things gave no inkling of how good the show would actually turn out to be.

(488)

Nancy is the name of the heroine in Wes Craven's A Nightmare On Elm Street. This is plainly no coincidence. Natalia Dyer said the Duffers asked her to watch A Nightmare On Elm Street in preparation for playing Nancy.

(489)

Dustin Henderson is the character with the third most amount of lines in season one of Stranger Things. Surprisingly, he has more dialogue in season one than Joyce and Hopper.

(490)

Terry Ives is the mother of Eleven/Jane Ives in Stranger Things. She took part in MKUltra experiments while in college. She was pregnant at the time but did not know this. Dr Brenner kidnapped her baby daughter for the unique abilities she was born with and then gave Terry electroconvulsive therapy which left her in a vegetative coma like state where she couldn't speak. Terry's sister Becky was told that Terry had suffered a miscarriage.

Aimee Mullins, who plays Terry Ives, was born with fibular hemimelia (missing fibula bones) and as a result had both of her legs amputated below the knee when she was one year old. Aimee competed in the Paralympics in 1996 in Atlanta.

(491)

The Duffer Brothers have said that the 2011 JJ Abrams film Super 8 was an influence on Stranger Things. Super 8 is set in the late 1970s and has a gang of children investigating a strange monster mystery in their small town. Super 8 was produced by Steven Spielberg and is very much a homage to Spielberg's Amblin films.

(492)

Shannon Purser was in a cinema with her mother watching a movie when the message came through on her phone telling her she had got the part of Barb Holland.

(493)

Mike Wheeler ranks fourth in Stranger Things when it comes to the total screentime given to characters in the three completed seasons.

(494)

The product visibility in Stranger Things 3 was valued at $15 million. There is no official product placement though.

Product placement is a form of advertising in which branded goods and services are featured in a production that targets a large audience.

(495)

The Duffer Brothers may have taken some inspiration for Stranger Things from the cult film Donnie Darko. In that movie the teenagers consult their teacher about portals and time travel.

(496)

After the first season of Stranger Things was a big hit in 2016, the kids in the cast went out trick or treating together at Halloween.

(497)

Finn Wolfhard, Noah Schnapp, Gaten Matarazzo, and Caleb McLaughlin competed in a 2017 episode of Spike's Lip Sync Battle.

(498)

The Palace Arcade in Stranger Things 2 is named after the 20 Grand Palace Arcade in the 1983 fantasy film WarGames.

WarGames stars Matthew Broderick as a whizz-kid teen who nearly starts World War III through his computer. The building used for the arcade was a derelict laundromat in Douglasville, Georgia. This building was absolutely filthy and had to be completely cleaned up. The games in the arcade were all real - though not period accurate because they have modern flat screens. The Palace Arcade in Stranger Things 2 has the popular machines Dragon's Lair, Dig Dug, Asteroids, Galaga, Centipede and Pac-Man.

Kids in the early eighties could play video games at home on things like the Commodore 64 and Atari but they were rather rudimentary - at least in comparison to what came later.

(499)

There would appear to be Alice in Wonderland easter eggs in Stranger Things. White Rabbit by Jefferson Airplane is heard when Eleven is in the diner in season one. When Hopper visits Terry Ives there is a picture of Alice in Jane's bedroom. The former could be a reference to LSD (which is part of MKUltra). The latter might simply be that Eleven is like Alice. Another connection is that Millie Bobby Brown played young Alice in ABC's Once Upon a Time in Wonderland (which was a spin-off from Once Upon a Time).

Alice's Adventures in Wonderland was published in 1865 and written by Lewis Carroll. Lewis Carroll was the pseudonym of Charles Dodgson. Dodgson was also a scholar, poet, and mathematician. He conjured up the adventures of Alice as a means to entertain the children of some friends during lazy summer days by the river. Once his fantastical tales were put into book form, Alice's Adventures in Wonderland eventually became of the most famous and enduring works of fiction ever published.

The book concerns a young girl named Alice who is dreamily sitting by a riverbank when she notices a white rabbit race past. Nothing strange about that you might think. However, this rabbit is wearing clothes and seems to keep checking a stopwatch as if time is of exceptional importance at this precise moment. Alice, naturally curious about this remarkable sight, explores but falls a down a rabbit hole into a strange world full of remarkable creatures who seem somewhat like the animals and insects of our world - only they can talk. It quickly transpires that logic plays little part in this topsy turvy and endlessly eccentric and strange world. But is it all a dream or is Alice really here?

Curiously, Alice's Adventures in Wonderland was not very well received when it first appeared and it was only after the publication of the sequel (Through the Looking Glass) that it got some traction and become much more loved and widely read. It's hard really to think of many more influential books than Alice's Adventures in Wonderland. It has inspired dozens of film and television adaptations and the image of little Alice in her blue dress is as identifiable as any character in fiction. Alice's Adventures in Wonderland is a delight on every page and fantastically weird and offbeat. The book is a wonderful celebration of nonsense and whimsy and full of preposterous conversations, memorable characters, puzzles, poems, and enjoyable absurdity.

(500)

Gaten Matarazzo thinks that Dustin Henderson is much cleverer and more academic than he is in real life. Gaten said the main difference between him and Dustin Henderson is that he is always trying to be funny whereas Dustin is funny without trying.

(501)

The Duffers suffered many rejections when they tried to pitch Montauk (eventually to become Stranger Things) in the entertainment industry. The Duffers later said that what seemed to put people off was the fact that this proposed show had a gang of children as major characters.

Network executives obviously didn't like this concept. The executives were completely wrong about this because, as much as anything, it WAS the kids that made Stranger Things so successful and popular.

(502)

A one-shot Stranger Things comic titled Stranger Things: Halloween Special, has Will Byers telling the boys a spooky story about a killer in Hawkins while they camp out in the woods at Castle Byers. This is one of the better Stranger Things comics because it's quite scary in places. It even has a few cuss words.

(503)

Randall Havens as Mr Clarke only has one scene in Stranger Things 3 because the season is set in the summer with the kids out of school.

(504)

The fact that Eleven was going to come back in Stranger Things 2 was such a big secret that Millie Bobby Brown wasn't even allowed to tell her family at first. This secret didn't last for long though.

(505)

The Weirdo On Maple Street appears to be a nod to a Rod Serling Twilight Zone episode called The Monsters Are Due on Maple Street. In this episode the residents of a usually peaceful and pleasant street descend into paranoia and witch hunts after a series of strange events which they suspect might involve aliens. Is one of them not who they appear to be?

The Monsters Are Due on Maple Street is a Rod Serling meditation on the need to remain civilised. The ensemble of actors work well together as tempers fray and while the science fiction coda is a little hokey it is a lot of fun in the best Twilight Zone tradition. The Monsters Are Due on Maple Street is based around one of Serling's frequent themes of how humanity needs to remain decent and kind if it is to have any future. Civilisation is a fragile thing. Could you count on your neighbour in a real crisis or would they simply be out for themselves and have no hesitation in turning on you? These are rich themes for a Twilight Zone story and work well in The Monsters Are Due on Maple Street.

This is enjoyably reminiscent of old science fiction classics like Invasion of the Body Snatchers and Invaders From Mars although the real monsters are of course ourselves rather than aliens. Very Cold War paranoia - something that The Twilight Zone and many science fiction writers tapped into at the time. There is of course a less than veiled subtext of McCarthyism in the story too with the people of Maple Street whipping themselves up into a frenzy and panic - that may or may not be completely misplaced - and looking for someone to blame. It's a clever rumination on paranoia and the nature of fear and how we always look for scapegoats when something goes wrong. Claude Atkins is solid as the central character Steve Brand. Brand wants to go into town but is warned that the power shortage is meant to isolate and contain the neighbourhood. It might be dangerous to leave. He isn't convinced though and not impressed by the increasing paranoia.

The story here has plenty to say about the inability of people to trust outsiders and think the worst of them. These all, sadly, remain timely themes. The atmosphere is this story is generated by the way electrical malfunctions signify something is wrong or unfathomable forces are at play. It's a device that everything from Close Encounters to Stranger Things has used in the decades that followed Maple Street's transmission. The Monsters are Due On Maple Street is a justifiably famous Twilight Zone episode and one that leaves plenty of food for thought.

(506)

Noah Schnapp said he really despises the signature bowl haircut of Will Byers and doesn't understand why Will has such a terrible hairstyle. Fortunately for Noah, he wears a wig to convey Will's hair and doesn't have to get a bowl haircut in real life.

Movie buffs think that Will's haircut could be a nod to the hairstyle of Barret Oliver as Bastian Balthazar Bux in The NeverEnding Story.

(507)

Gaten Matarazzo did his first Stranger things audition in New York. He was eventually flown to Los Angeles to do a final test. As part of his final auditions for Stranger Things, Gaten had to perform a scene with Finn Wolfhard to see what their chemistry was like. Their chemistry was obviously great in the audition because they were both cast in the show.

(508)

Around three hundred female child actors read for the part of Eleven before they found Millie Bobby Brown. It was a tricky part to cast because child actors can easily lose focus and concentration when they don't have much dialogue. The Duffers said they looked at nearly a THOUSAND boys before the parts of Mike, Will, Lucas, and Dustin were cast. The world of child acting can be a rough old business. Child actors have to compete with literally hundreds of other children for parts.

(509)

A lot of people wonder if Millie Bobby Brown actually likes Eggo waffles in real life. The answer seems to be that she doesn't mind them but they aren't something she would personally go out of her way to purchase. Millie said that the Eggo eating scenes in season one were not amazingly pleasant because the waffles were not very fresh. She did though have a 'spit bucket' for food scenes. This is something of a necessity because actors obviously don't want to end up eating endless amounts of food because of retakes.

Millie said that it was much worse shooting the scene where Eleven eats the fries in Benny's diner because the fries were cold and congealed.

(510)

In the third season of Stranger Things you can make out an illustration of Bob Newby on the fridge depicted as a superhero.

(511)

The real location for the Hawkins Community Pool in season three was 2171 Lakewood Avenue, Atlanta, GA. This is South Bend pool. The pool was quite close to the studio where Stranger Things is made so proved to be a convenient location. It was quite hot when they shot some of the pool stuff and Dacre Montgomery ended up with sunburn because of his lifeguard scenes as Billy Hargrove.

(512)

In the Stranger Things season one finale, Eleven is exhausted after dispatching the agents in the corridor and has to be carried into the school classroom by Dustin. In the script it is Mike who carries Eleven but Finn Wolfhard found it too difficult to run and carry Millie Bobby Brown at the same time so they had to abandon this plan. Gaten Matarazzo - despite having an injured ankle at the time - had no such trouble and so it is Dustin who carries Eleven in the finale.

(513)

Dragon's Lair plays a big part in anticipating the story of

Stranger Things 2. This is a laserdisc video game published by Cinematronics in 1983. The game was unique because it featured animation by ex-Disney animator Don Bluth. It was a lavish and enticing looking game and had the player taking the role of Dirk the Daring, a knight attempting to rescue Princess Daphne from the evil dragon Singe. However, the game was not a game in the sense that other arcade games were games. In Dragon's Lair you made a series of choices and then watched what happened to Dirk next as a consequence of your choice. It was sort of like a 'choose your fate' adventure rather than the joystick waggling, button pressing action romp gamers were used to playing.

The Duffers said they never liked Dragon's Lair but they included it in Stranger Things 2 because the animation looks cool. Dragon's Lair didn't have the long lasting appeal that Bluth might have hoped (although it was ported to numerous home gaming systems with varying degrees of success) and wasn't the industry game changer it seemed to be at the time but - for a brief moment - Dragon's Lair was all the rage and the main attraction of arcades in the early eighties.

(514)

The dummy of the 'dead' Will Byers in season one that Hopper cuts into after he breaks into the morgue was built by Justin Raleigh. Raleigh's work is so realistic that Boston Children's Hospital use his dummies for surgeons to train with. David Harbour said it was 'gross' cutting into the dummy because it seemed so real. The dummy of Will Byers was used again in season two during the cabin scene with the hot poker.

The Duffer Brothers actually showed Noah Schnapp's mother the realistic Will Byers dummy for a joke. That was a bit macabre but luckily she saw the funny side.

(515)

Paul Reiser agreed to play Dr Owens in Stranger Things 2 even before any scripts were available to read. Reiser is primarily a comedian and comic actor but sci-fi and horror buffs know him best as Carter Burke in the classic Alien sequel Aliens. Carter Burke was the insincere company man who pretended to be nice but was really trying to sabotage the mission so that he could secure some Xenomorph specimens for the sinister company.

The first appearance of Owens in Stranger Things (where he's giving Will Byers a medical check at the lab) deliberately mimics the first introduction to Carter Burke in Aliens (where he visits Riply in her hospital bed at Gateway Station).

Paul Reiser said that when he started shooting his scenes for Stranger Things 2 he genuinely had no idea if Dr Owens was going to be a goodie or a baddie because he hadn't seen all of the scripts.

The scene near the end of Stranger Things 2 where Owens gives Hopper half of his sandwich at the diner is a reference to Reiser's character in the cult 1982 film Diner. Reiser played a character in Diner who is always asking people if they are going to finish the last half of their sandwich.

(516)

A serving of two Eggo waffles has 194.6 calories.

(517)

It took 27 motors on the Demogorgon costume to open and close the fanged petal like face of the creature.

(518)

Matthew Modine and Millie Bobby Brown both think that Dr Brenner is not as evil as seems to be. Maybe they think he's just misunderstand!

(519)

Katheryn Naranjo, who edited the season three finale, said the most complex scene to edit was the final fight between Hopper and Grigori.

(520)

The Ranker website voted the Stranger Things Back to the 90s Trivial Pursuit as the best board game inspired by the show.

(521)

Kyle Dixon and Michael Stein said that one of their first duties on Stranger Things was to come up with a demo of the music theme for the character of Eleven.

(522)

The Duffer Brothers said it was a great relief when they found Millie Bobby Brown because they were struggling to find a child actor capable of the raw emotion necessary to play Eleven.

(523)

When the first season of Stranger Things came out, Gaten Matarazzo described his character Dustin as a gregarious, foul-mouthed twelve-year-old boy.

(524)

You can now, should you wish, buy a Demogorgan Baby Bonnet.

(525)

Michael Park, who plays Tom in Stranger Things 3, is yet another actor on the show with Broadway connections.

(526)

Universal Studios' Halloween Horror Nights created a creepy Stranger Things maze in 2019.

(527)

Steve Harrington has a little holster for his ice-cream scooper in Stranger Things 3.

This was an amusing idea by the costume department.

(528)

Eleven's pant suspenders in season three of Stranger Things appear to be a reference to Robin Williams in the sitcom Mork & Mindy.

(529)

In the initial plans for Montauk, those who encountered the Demogorgon were going to bleed from the eyes and ears simply by being in close proximity to the creature.

(530)

For the death scene of Barb Holland, Shannon Purser had crew members pulling her ankles to convey the Demogorgon tugging her down into the swimming pool in the Harrington house. Shawn Levy was one of these crew members at one point.

(531)

The Stranger Things 3 videogame has a rating of 62% on Metacritic.

(532)

In the pitch document for Montauk, Mike Wheeler travels into the Upside Down to search for Will Byers. This was obviously something that never happened in the show though when Stranger Things made it onto the screen.

(533)

In Dungeons & Dragons, the Demogorgon has a tail that functions like a whip and can drain the life force out of its foes.

(534)

A fun but improbable fan theory is that Stranger Things takes place in the same universe as Stephen King's books. One problem with this theory is that we've seen characters in the show reading Stephen King books. The trooper that Hopper punches in the morgue in season one was reading Cujo.

(535)

Paul Reiser is the richest member of the Stranger Things cast. He's said to be worth about $40 million.

(536)

The Farrah Fawcett hairspray so beloved of Steve and Dustin stopped being produced in 1984.

The props department couldn't find a real can of this vintage product so they had to replicate the packaging instead.

(537)

Natalia Dyer combined appearing in the early seasons of Stranger Things with being a student at New York University

(538)

Hopper's Hawaiian shirt in season three was made by the costume department from 20 yards of vintage '80s fabric.

(539)

Karen Wheeler is reading Johanna Lindsey's romance novel Heart of Thunder in the bath when Billy Hargrove knocks on the door in Stranger Things 2. The two lovers on the cover of the book are illustrated to resemble Karen and Billy.

(540)

Hopper visits Merril's farm to investigate the pumpkin patch mystery in Stranger Things 2. Merril is the name of a character in two Stephen King stories - Needful Things and The Body.

(541)

Costume designer Kimberly Adams-Galligan created 'mood boards' to design the clothes each character wears in season one. Mood boards are basically sketches and illustrations of the characters so that the costume designers can get a clear picture of what they are going to look like in the show.

There were a lot of factors that went into the clothes - including social class. The clothes of Will Byers, for example, were designed to have a more worn hand-me down quality. Mike Wheeler, by contrast, comes from a fairly well off family financially so his clothes were newer.

(542)

When Alexei is at the fair in Stranger Things 3, a clown walks past him with a Gremlins puppet. You can also see some Fraggle figures as prizes. Fraggle Rock was a Jim Henson television show in the vein of The Muppets.

(543)

A four issue Stranger Things comic titled The Tomb of Ybwen is set between seasons two and three and has Will Byers embarking on a snowbound quest in memory of Bob Newby. This comic is passable enough - most notably because it supplies Mr Clarke with a bigger and more heroic role than he has on the television show.

(544)

Hasbro released a Dungeons & Dragons game based on Stranger Things. The game included two Demogorgon figures, six Polyhedral dice, and five character sheets.

(545)

The full list of songs used in season one of Stranger Things is -

(THE VANISHING OF WILL BYERS) Can't Seem to Make You Mine by The Seeds, She Has Funny Cars by Jefferson Airplane, I Shall Not Care by Pearls Before Swine, Jenny May by Trader Horne, Every Little Bit by Jackie James and Jackie Curnow, White Rabbit by Jefferson Airplane, Africa by Toto.

(THE WEIRDO ON MAPLE STREET) Go Nowhere by Reagan Youth, Should I Stay or Should I Go by The Clash, Deck The Halls by Chicks With Hits, Jingle Bells by The Canterbury Choir, Dark Stars by Mark Glass, I'm Taking Off (Shield Your Eyes) by Space Knife, Body Language by Alexander Baker & Clair Mario, Tie A Yellow Ribbon by Brotherhood of Man, Raise A Little Hell by Trooper, I Melt With You by Modern English, Hazy Shade Of Winter by The Bangles.

(HOLLY,JOLLY) Waiting for a Girl Like You by Foreigner, We Wish You a Merry Christmas by Joel Evans & Friends, Brahm's Lullaby by Johannes Brahms, Heroes sung by Peter Gabriel (original song by David Bowie).

(THE BODY) Atmosphere by Joy Division, Should I Stay or Should I Go by The Clash, Color Dreams by The Deep.

(THE FLEA AND THE ACROBAT) Elegia by New Order, Green Desert by Tangerine Dream, Nocturnal Me by Echo & The Bunnymen.

(THE MONSTER) The Bargain Store by Dolly Parton & Kenny Rogers, Sunglasses at Night by Corey Hart, I See the Future by Andrew Pinching, Exit by Tangerine Dream, Happy José by Kookie Freeman, Brahm's Lullaby by Johannes Brahm.

(THE BATHTUB) Fields of Coral by Vangelis, Should I Stay or Should I Go by The Clash.

(THE UPSIDE DOWN) Horizon (Warsaw Gate Mix) by Tangerine Dream, When It's Cold I'd Like to Die by Moby, Carol of the Bells by Mormon Tabernacle Choir, White Christmas by Bing Crosby.

(546)

39% of people who play Dungeons & Dragons are female.

(547)

Benny's Burgers is in reality Tiffany's Kitchen in Lithia Springs, Georgia.

(548)

The Soviet doctor who tortures Steve in Stranger Things 3 is named Dr Zharkov. Dr Zarkov is a famous character in Flash Gordon.

(549)

Charlie Heaton said that in the original scripts he got for season one of Stranger Things, Jonathan and Nancy became a couple quite quickly. These plans were obviously changed though by the desire of the Duffers to give Steve Harrington a chance to redeem himself.

(550)

Steve climbing up to Nancy's bedroom using the outside of the house in season one is a nod to similar scenes in the Wes Craven films A Nightmare On Elm Street and Scream.

(551)

The Demogorgon seems to have powers of blood detection - which would make it rather like a shark.

(552)

Most of the storylines for Stranger Things 2 had already been worked out by the Duffers before they even wrote any scripts. They came out of season one with plenty of ideas for what would happen next if the show continued.

They already knew they wanted to put Eleven and Hopper together and have Will Byers still troubled by his lingering connection to the Upside Down.

(553)

On season one of Stranger Things, the editors changed the aspect ratio on certain scenes to give them more of an eighties movie feel.

(554)

In the Stranger Things tie-in novel, Stranger Things: Suspicious Minds, Eleven is named after the anthropologist Jane Goodall.

(555)

The sound effects designer (Craig Henigan) on Stranger Things says that for scenes in the Upside Down his main focus is on spooky creaking noises!

(556)

General Mills released some limited edition Stranger Things cereals in 2021. Limited edition boxes of Cinnamon Toast Crunch, Cheerios and Lucky Charms were given Upside Down makeovers.

(557)

The Gamer website ranked the Dead By Daylight Stranger Things crossover as the best game the show has inspired so far. Dead by Daylight is a survival horror asymmetric multiplayer online game. In the Dead By Daylight Stranger Things crossover the characters of Steve Harrington and Nancy Wheeler are involved.

(558)

In 2021, Netflix's Ted Sarandos seemed to suggest that he saw Stranger Things as a franchise that was only just beginning. His comments seem to imply that Netflix want to do some Stranger Things spin-off shows when the base show ends.

(559)

You can now buy a BrickHeadz LEGO double-pack which features the Demogorgon and Eleven. The characters comprise 192 pieces and will set you back $19.99.

(560)

A video game which influenced the Duffer Brothers on Stranger Things was Dark Souls - part of the Souls franchise.

Dark Souls takes place in the fictional kingdom of Lordran, where players assume the role of a cursed undead character who begins a pilgrimage to discover the fate of their kind. It was the palpable atmosphere of dread in the game which the Duffers wanted to transplant to the horror scenes in Stranger Things.

(561)

David Harbour said he would like Hopper to have more scenes with Steve Harrington because he thinks they would make a funny duo. Joe Keery is obviously popular because Finn Wolfhard said he would also like Mike Wheeler to have more scenes with Steve.

(562)

The survey site YouGov reported that 10% of British Netflix subscribers binged the entire second season of Stranger Things in one day.
(563)

Alec Utgoff, who plays Alexei in Stranger Things 3, was born in Kiev in what was then the Soviet Union but is now Ukraine. Utgoff moved to London when he was eleven.

(564)

Eleven owns some Sweet Valley High books in season three. Sweet Valley High is a series of young adult novels attributed to American author Francine Pascal (who used a team of ghostwriters) that began in 1983. The books were later adapted into a television show of the same name that ran from 1994 to 1997.

The books and TV show revolve around the lives of two young twin girls who live in Sweet Valley, California.

(565)

The films of Edgar Wright were an influence on the sound effects in Stranger Things.

(566)

The Demogorgon would appear to have powers of telekinesis because we saw a door unlocking when Will was trying to hide from it in the first ever episode of Stranger Things.

(567)

Noah Schnapp is given surprisingly little to do in season three apart from occasionally feel the back of his neck to indicate the Mind Flayer is active. It's understandable that they wanted to give poor Will Byers a break after all that he's been through but given how good Schnapp was in season two it seems strange that he wasn't given more to do in Stranger Things 3. We definitely miss the Will/Jonathan scenes - notable by their absence in Stranger Things 3.

(568)

When Robin and Steve are tied up together in the base in season three it feels a lot like a riff on Indy and his father tied up in Indiana Jones and the Last Crusade.

(569)

Stranger Things 3 is a more stand alone season than Stranger Things 2.

The second season still had a number of loose ends to tie up and had to deal with the ramifications of Barb's death and Will's time trapped in the upside Down. Stranger Things 2 also had to show us how Eleven survived the classroom battle with the Demogorgon and came to be living with Hopper. Stranger Things 3, by contrast, had more of a clean slate to do whatever it wanted to.

(570)

Dustin's cymbal-clapping monkey toy that comes to life (thanks to Eleven) in Stranger Things 3 could refer to Stephen King's short story The Monkey.

(571)

The voices of the boys got deeper during the course of shooting season one because they were going through puberty. This created some problems for the sound editing.

(572)

The scene in season two were Max is driving a car but can't reach the pedals is based on a similar sequence involving Indy's sidekick 'Short Round' in Indiana Jones and the Temple of Doom.

(573)

Millie Bobby Brown said that she mostly learned how to do an American accent by watching an awful lot of Hannah Montana.

(574)

The Upside Down seems to exist in the same space as our own world. Our biggest evidence for this is the fact that Will - in the Upside Down Byers house - was able to communicate with his mother through the lights. He was clearly in the same 'space' as Joyce if not in the same dimension.

(575)

The Stranger Things editors and producers say they sometimes leave a few 'flubs' in if they think it adds to the scene.

Examples of this are Brett Gelman dropping scrambled egg when Murray has breakfast with Jonathan and Nancy in season two. Another example is when Natalia Dyer ended up with punch dribbling down her chin during the Halloween party scene in Stranger Things 2. Nancy was supposed to be a bit sozzled so this unintended detail actually made sense.

(576)

One of the reasons the Duffer Brothers chose Kyle Dixon and Mike Stein to do the music for Stranger Things was because they didn't want to hire an established composer whose music the audience would already be familiar with.

(577)

Eleven pointing to the picture of the missing Will in season one is a nod (whether conscious or unconscious) to a scene from the 1985 film Witness when Lucas Haas points to Danny Glover's picture in the police station.

(578)

In season two, Dr Owens speaks to Jonathan and Nancy about the danger of the Upside Down falling into the hands of others. By this he obviously means the Soviet Union. You could say then that this scene anticipates the plot of season three.

(579)

The Duffer Brothers and Shawn Levy say that not every alleged homage or Easter egg in Stranger Things is deliberate.

They say that occasionally they are even accused of doing a homage to a movie that they haven't even heard of!

(580)

The script for the season three finale was thirty pages longer than any other episode in Stranger Things 3. This is because there was so much action and mayhem to describe.

(581)

Benny gives Eleven some strawberry ice cream in The Vanishing of Will Byers while he waits (or so he presumes) for social services to arrive. Although Eleven is seen to be enjoying the ice cream, Millie Bobby Brown did not.

Millie said she doesn't care much for strawberry ice-cream. They used strawberry because it looked better on screen than vanilla or chocolate.

(582)

Joe Keery said he hurt his back shooting the junkyard sequence in Stranger Things 2 where Steve and some of the kids are trapped in the old rusted bus by DemoDogs. He had to do multiple takes of a scene where Steve has to jump into the bus and these obviously took their toll.

(583)

The production designers on Stranger Things 3 had a nice stroke of luck when they found a folder that included many photographs of Gwinnett Place Mall as it was in the eighties.

(584)

The Duffer Brothers said the alien queen in the 1986 film Aliens was an influence on the Mind Flayer in that they wanted the Upside Down to have a big boss in the way that alien queen is the boss of the aliens.

(585)

Matty Cardarople has a spit bucket in the show for when Keith eats Cheetos so that his mouth doesn't get clogged up or turn orange.

(586)

David Harbour said that he looked a lot like Joe Keery when he was very young.

(587)

Thirteen hours of music was written for season one. Not all of this could be used because there were only eight episodes.

(588)

In an IGN poll, the first season of Stranger Things was voted the greatest season. It earned 53% of all the votes.

(589)

A man named Al Bielek claimed him and his brother were participants in experiments in Camp Hero and developed psychic powers. When they decided to escape, Bielek claims his brother produced a monster from his subconscious which ran amok and forced the project to be closed down and covered up. One can easily see how the (rather fanciful) legends surrounding Camp Hero in Montauk partly inspired what became Stranger Things.

(590)

The novel Stranger Things: Suspicious Minds by Gwenda Bond reconfigures the Stranger Things universe - at least in relation to what we already knew. In this tie-in novel, encounters with the Upside Down are shown to predate Eleven.

Suspicious Minds revolves around a young Terry Ives and tells the story of how she came to volunteer for LSD experiments under Dr Brenner in 1969 while a student.

(591)

A company released a six foot Demogorgon Yard Sprinkler.

(592)

There were nearly 5,000 digital special effect shots in the first two seasons of Stranger Things.

(593)

The 1979 Russian science fiction film Stalker by Andrei Tarkovsky is about a mysterious restricted area known as the Zone.

This concept was an influence on the Upside Down in Stranger Things.

(594)

In Stranger Things 3, Mr Clarke has a table top town model. Table top models feature in Die Hard, Back to the Future, and Beetlejuice.

(595)

Dacre Montgomery was twenty-two years-old when he was cast as Billy Hargrove.

(596)

CCTV style footage named Hawkins Monitored was released to promote Stranger Things 2 in which you could secretly watch characters from the show.

(597)

Season one offers a nice twist on the teen romance tropes of eighties movies in that Nancy ends the season with Steve rather than Jonathan.

(598)

In his book The Montauk Project, Preston Nichols claimed that Camp Hero had an experiment called Project Rainbow which was designed to open up an alternate dimension.

(599)

The Duffer Brothers and David Harbour have admitted that they were never terribly convincing in that brief period when they pretended to be uncertain about whether Hopper was really dead or not after Stranger Things 3.

You didn't need to be Sherlock Holmes to deduce that Hopper would be back.

(600)

Millie Bobby Brown said she doesn't really know what Eleven's fashion style is because Eleven doesn't know herself. Eleven is obviously not what you would describe as a fashion obsessed girl.

(601)

One of the Netflix sound stages caught fire during the production of Stranger Things 4. Thankfully, no one was injured.

(602)

The Duffer Brothers said they had already conceived the story in season two where Nancy seeks to get justice for Barb even before season one was released and Barb Holland became a popular character.

(603)

The cinema in Hawkins is showing the Tom Cruise film All the Right Moves in season one. In season two it is playing The Terminator.

(604)

Finn Wolfhard as Mike Wheeler had 199 less lines in season two than in season one.

(605)

It is surely no coincidence that Spielberg's E.T. and Stranger Things both have characters names Mike and Steve.

(606)

Millie Bobby Brown thinks that Eleven should never be called Jane (which is her real name). Millie prefers Eleven or El.

(607)

Will's terrifying encounters with the Mind Flayer - especially the scene where he wanders to the door of his house - is a very obvious homage to Spielberg's Close Encounters of the Third Kind.

(608)

There is a costume Easter egg near the end of Stranger Things 3 when Lucas and Max wear outfits worn by Eric and Donna in 'That 70s Show.

(609)

The depiction of the Soviet Union is very comic book and (classic) James Bond in Stranger Things 3. They have pristine clean uniforms, high technology, and are capable of constructing complex clandestine bases in the United States without anyone from the intelligence services noticing.

In reality, the Soviet Union in 1985 was only five years away from collapsing and an impoverished state struggling to fund its outsized military.

(610)

Eleven falling into Mike's arms after Eleven battles Billy in The Sauna Test episode of Stranger Things 3 was not in the script but something Millie Bobby Brown did on instinct. The director Shawn Levy liked this improvisation and kept it in the episode.

(611)

In the season three finale, Dustin and Suzy perform the theme song to the 1984 fantasy film The Neverending Story. The original theme song was sung by Limahl with Beth Anderson. Limahl had never heard of Stranger Things but said his nephew got super excited when he told him the song was going to be in the show.

Downloads and streams of the song rocketed by 800% when Stranger Things 3 came out. Gaten Matarazzo and Gabriella Pizzolo both wore an earpiece during the song so they could hear one another and match their harmonies. The Duffers were initially going to have Dustin and Suzie sing the Ent song from Lord Of The Rings but they axed this plan when they heard that Amazon were making a television show based on Lord of the Rings. The Duffers presumably didn't want Amazon to think that Netflix were being cheeky with a Lord of the Rings joke.

(612)

The full list of songs used in Stranger Things 2 are -

(MADMAX) Whip It by Devo, Just Another Day by Oingo Boingo, Talking in Your Sleep by The Romantics, Rock You Like a Hurricane by Scorpions, Spooky Movies by Gary Paxton, Every Other Girl by Prehistoric Wolves.

(TRICK OR TREAT, FREAK) Ghostbusters by Ray Parker Jr., Wango Tango by Ted Nugent, Blackout by Swing Set, Shout at the Devil by Mötley Crüe, Islands in the Stream by Kenny Rogers & Dolly Parton, Monster Mash by Bobby Boris Pickett, Girls On Film by Duran Duran, Outside the Realm by Big Giant Circles.

(THE POLLYWOG) Whistle On the River by The Mercy Brothers, You Don't Mess Around with Jim by Jim Croce, Go! by Tones On Tail, The Ghost in You by The Psychedelic Furs, Clean Cut American Kid by III Repute, Cookin' by Al Casey Combo, How I Feel About You by Jumpstreet.

(WILL THE WISE) This Is Radio Clash by The Clash, Scarface (Push It To the Limit) by Paul Engemann, The Growing by The Haxan Cloak.

(DIG DUG) Try My Love by Carroll Lloyd, You Ought To Be With Me by Carl Weathers, Green, Green Grass of Home by Bobby Bare, Can I Do What I Want by Shock Therapy, Metal Sport by Hittman, Darling Don't Leave Me by Robert Görl, When the Sun Goes Down by The Jetzons, Strenght in Numbers by Channel 3, Open the Kingdom (Liquid Days, Part II) by Philip Glass Ensemble, Douglas Perry, Michael Riesman & Michael Reisman, No More by Billie Holiday.

(THE SPY) Hammer to Fall by Queen, Where Django's At by Cameron Brooks, There Is Frost On the Moon by Artie Shaw and His Orchestra, You Better Go Now by Billie Holiday, Blue Bayou by Roy Orbinson, Round and Round by Ratt.

(THE LOST SISTER) Runaway by Bon Jovi, Outside the Realm by Big Giant Circles, Back To Nature by Fad Gadget, The Bank Robbery by John Carpenter, Dead End Justice by The Runaways, Whisper to a Scream (Birds Fly) by The Icicle Works.

(THE MIND FLAYER) The Love You Save (May Be Your Own) by Jack Cook, The Four Horseman by Metallica, Should I Stay or Should I Go by The Clash.

(THE GATE) The Way We Were - Barbara Streisand, I Do Believe (I Fell in Love) by Donna Summer, I See Charcoal (You See Scarlet) by Cameron Brooks, Rare Bird by Tangerine Dream, Jingle Bells Rock by Bobby Helms, Love is a Battlefield by Pat Benatar, Twist of Fate by Olivia Newton John, Time After Time by Cyndi Lauper, Every Breath You Take by The Police.

(613)

Dustin's new invention in Stranger Things 3 deliberately looks like Randall Peltzer's electric hammer from Joe Dante's 1984 film Gremlins.

(614)

Millie Bobby Brown had no idea in her Stranger Things auditions that Eleven was going to have super powers nor that she would be playing a major character in the show. Millie would later say she had assumed Eleven was going to be a minor sidekick.

Millie's first auditions for Stranger Things were done on Skype and made up of special scenes created solely for her screen tests. Millie said she had to do several further auditions for the part of Eleven. In the end she was flown to Los Angeles for screen tests. At this point she deduced that she must be quite close to getting the part if they were taking the time and expense to fly her across the Atlantic.

(615)

Joe Keery initially tested for the part of Jonathan Byers. When he did his audition to play Steve Harrington he had to do the scene where Steve smashes Jonathan's camera.
Joe had to do extensive swimming training to play Steve because he was told that Steve Harrington was going to be a champion swimmer at school. In the end though this idea seemed to be jettisoned and all that swimming training wasn't necessary.

(616)

The location where the children walk the train tracks in the woods in season one is Stone Mountain Park in Georgia.

(617)

According to The Hawkins Middle School Yearbook/Hawkins High School Yearbook, the ambition of Will Byers is to be a comic book artist.

(618)

Millie Bobby Brown said The Bathtub is her favourite season one episode of Stranger Things. There's an awful lot to love in The Bathtub despite it being a quieter sort of episode (save for the big chase sequence at the start). It's great to see Mike and Lucas shake hands and make up at the beginning after their argument, and it's also great to see Winona Ryder and Millie Bobby Brown get some scenes together.

(619)

Finn Wolfhard says that, unlike his Stranger Things co-stars, he isn't very good at pranks.

(620)

The triple-decker Eggo extravaganza that Hopper prepares for Eleven in season two has whipped cream, Hershey's Kisses, Reese's Pieces and Mike and Ike candies. Ikes are oblong fruit-flavored chewy candies.

(621)

Maya Hawke as Robin has the sixth most amount of screentime out of any character in season three. This is rather impressive given that Robin is a new character. Robin has more screentime than Mike, Nancy, Jonathan, Max, and Lucas.

(622)

Bob Newby is supposed to be 37 years-old in Stranger Things 2. Sean Astin was about a decade older though in real life.

(623)

In some of the discarded original concept art for the look of the Demogorgon the creature has huge oversized clawed arms and hairs and moss on scaly green skin. It looks rather like a nightmarish cross between the Hulk and Swamp Thing.

(624)

Millie Bobby Brown said her parents were actually a big help in coming up with the body language she developed to play Eleven in season one. They gave her some helpful coaching and feedback.

(625)

The cast were allowed to do some free shopping at the Starcourt Mall near the end of shooting on season three although the expensive period authentic sneakers were off limits because they were only on loan.

Sadie Sink filled up a goodie bag from the mall but then left it in her trailer. One would hope she managed to get that bag in the end!

Sadie said she mostly picked out a lot of scented candles from the mall to put in her bag.

(626)

Bob Newby's nickname Bob the Brain might be a reference to Bobby "The Brain" Heenan. Heenan was a famous wrestling manager in the 1980s.

(627)

For the boys quest (Operation Mirkwood) to find Will in season one, Dustin brings Nutty Bars, Bazooka bubble gum, Pez, Smarties, Pringles, Nilla Wafers, an apple and trail mix.

(628)

Millie Bobby Brown was eleven years-old when she was cast as Eleven.

(629)

Jonathan Byers had the sixth most amount of screentime for any character in season one.

However, in season three he ranked only thirteenth when it came to screentime.

(630)

In the birth certificate that Dr Owens gives Hopper at the end of season two (so that Hopper can adopt Eleven), her name on the certificate is Jane Hopper and it states she was born in Hawkins.

(631)

Sadie Sink first met Gaten Matarazzo and Caleb McLaughlin at a park in New York where all the Broadway kids would go to play between shows.

(632)

The Duffer Brothers said they tried to be quite sparing when it came to the use of flashbacks in Stranger Things because this device has become somewhat rote and over familiar in television.

(633)

Millie Bobby Brown said it was a bit weird to have to do a kissing scene for the season two finale in front of about 200 extras and crew members.

(634)

Eggo waffles come in a variety of different flavours.

These include pumpkin spice, cinnamon and brown sugar, chocolate chip muffin, strawberry shortcake, cinnamon toast, and chocolate chip banana.

(635)

Pac-Man was the most popular machine among the crew when they played the games in the Palace Arcade set.

(636)

Gaten Matarazzo says he is probably the biggest nerd in the Stranger Things cast although he thinks that Finn Wolfhard runs him pretty close.

(637)

The character of Kali was going to be a thirtysomething man named Roman in the early plans for season two.

(638)

There is a Quentin Tarantino reference in The Bathtub when Jonathan's car trunk is opened. Tarantino often has a similar trunk scene in his films.

(639)

Millie Bobby Brown, who has been in two Godzilla movies lest we forget, doesn't think Eleven would win in a battle against Godzilla.

(640)

Erica Sinclair has a sunflower and rainbow on her wall in season two. A sunflower and rainbow are the keys to understanding the catatonic state of Terry Ives.

This connection seems to be merely a little mischief Easter egg that doesn't really mean anything significant.

(641)

In modern Dungeons & Dragons lore, the Demogorgon is described as the embodiment of chaos, madness, and destruction.

(642)

Mike Wheeler's calculator watch in season one is an Alpha Calc Chrono.

They wanted Mike to wear an E.T watch but they couldn't get the rights.

(643)

According to entertainment sites, Sadie Sink was paid
$150,000 an episode on Stranger Things 3. This would put her
below the salary of the other teens in the show. Presumably
this was because the others had been in the show longer than
Sadie?

(644)

Dacre Montgomery took home one of Billy Hargrove's tank
tops as a memento when shooting on Stranger Things 3 ended.

(645)

Gaten Matarazzo says that being in Stranger Things is the
coolest job on earth.

(646)

Finn Wolfhard said he found Stranger Things quite scary when
he watched it for the first time.

(647)

What happened to the DemoDog that Dustin put in the fridge
near the end of season two? This is never mentioned in
Stranger Things 3.

(648)

The large ensemble cast in Stranger Things is a strength in
that there are any number of characters who could feasibly be
given a larger role (and any number of hitherto untapped
potential partnerships and dynamics) but it does have a
downside. The downside is that there is not enough room to
give everyone the amount of dialogue and scenes they might
deserve.

(649)

Terry Ives can't speak, save for repeating the same few words over and over - "Breathe. Sunflower. Rainbow. Three to the right. Four to the left. 450."

The reason for these repeating words is as follows; 'Breathe' was Terry giving birth. 'Sunflower' was a vase she awoke to. 'Rainbow' was a child's room she found in the Hawkins Lab. 'Three to the right, four to the left' was the safe combination she used to get a gun so that she could go to the lab and get Jane back. '450' was the voltage of the treatment Brenner gave her to ensure her silence.

(650)

3 Musketeers is a candy bar made by Mars, Incorporated. Introduced in 1932, it is a candy bar consisting of chocolate-covered fluffy whipped nougat. In Europe you might know this as a Milky Way. Dustin feeds his new pet 'Dart' 3 Musketeers candy.

(651)

Billy giving Steve a rough time on the basketball court in Stranger Things 2 is a homage to the eighties Michael J Fox comedy Teen Wolf.

(652)

When Eleven is watching television alone in the cabin in Stranger Things 2 she imitates Susan Lucci while watching All My Children. You can definitely detect Millie Bobby Brown's real life English accent in this scene.

(653)

Lucas brings binoculars, an army knife, a hammer, a camouflage bandanna, and a Wrist-Rocket slingshot for the boys Mirkwood quest to find Will in season one.

(654)

Stranger Things 2 takes place during an election. Ted Wheeler has a Ronald Reagan placard in his garden. Dustin's mother is clearly a Democrat as she has a Walter Mondale placard.

(655)

Scoops Ahoy was inspired by Baskin-Robbins.

(656)

A whopping 37% of Eleven's lines in Stranger Things 2 come from The Lost Sister alone.

(657)

Gaten Matarazzo said that a lot of his own food obsessions were written into the character of Dustin Henderson.

(658)

The Duffers said that Mr Clarke essentially functions as the eighties version of Wikipedia in season one of Stranger Things. It's a handy device to have a teacher character who can explain the science of what might be happening in Hawkins to the boys - and thus the audience too.

(659)

Gaten Matarazzo says that Stranger Things 4 is his favourite season when it comes to the clothes and costumes that Dustin Henderson has to wear.

(660)

Comic con built a shrine to Barb and the Duffers joked that the last ever shot in Stranger Things should be Barb's hand reaching up through her grave. Shannon Purser later got a part in the TV show Riverdale so she didn't do too badly in the end - despite the brief nature of her contribution to Stranger Things.

(661)

The scenes of Eleven in the lab in season one are very inspired by Firestarter - a Stephen King novel which was turned into a 1984 film with Drew Barrymore.

Firestarter is about a little girl named Charlie with pyrokinetic flame inducing powers (which she gained from her parents participating in Project MKltra type experiments). Charlie wears lab brain sensors on her head in the film like Eleven does in Stranger Things in the lab.

The film version of Firestarter is rather forgotten these days. Trivia - John Carpenter was supposed to direct Firestarter but got the axe when The Thing bombed. Though it is lauded as a classic today, critics hated The Thing back in 1982. After he was fired from Firestarter, Carpenter instead directed an adaptation of Stephen King's Christine. You can see many Christine influences in Stranger Things. Billy Hargrove, for example, has the same car as Christine's villain Buddy Repperton. They both have a Camero.

(662)

Gaten Matarazzo's family run a diner called Matarazzo's Pizzeria and Restaurant in New Jersey. Gaten's fame has been a boost for business because Stranger Things fans often visit in the hope of seeing Gaten there. He does actually help out at the Pizzeria when he isn't busy acting.

(663)

There is an Eggo card game based on Stranger Things.

(664)

The radio Hopper and Eleven keep in contact on in Stranger Things 2 is tuned to broadcast channel 11.

(665)

Shawn Levy said that the idea of throwing Erica in with Steve's gang and trapping them in a Soviet military base in season three was so crazy that they simply had to do it.

(666)

Stranger Things 3 leans heavily on season one in terms of its story. Like the first season, Stranger Things 3 has at its heart a conspiracy that the characters must, in their own ways through separate investigations, uncover.

Just as in season one, Hopper is slow to detect the conspiracy and must be prodded into action by Joyce Byers.

(667)

Eleven is the number most associated with faith and psychics.

(668)

In the scripts for Stranger Things, the other dimension was known as the 'Nether'. At some point it was decided that the 'Upside Down' was more catchy.

(669)

The Montauk conspiracies mostly derive from The Montauk Project book by Preston Nichols. Nichols claims to have become involved with Montauk in 1968 and trained children to be "PSI Warriors".

The claims of Preston Nichols are not taken terribly seriously.

He couldn't even supply any evidence that he had a science or engineering degree - despite claiming to be an expert in electronics.

(670)

Justice for Barb was a movement that sprung up in fandom concerning the early demise of Barb Holland - victim of the Upside Down in Steve Harrington's swimming pool. The main driver of the movement was the observation that - Nancy aside - no one in the show seemed to notice or care much that Barb had suddenly vanished without trace.

(671)

One of the final nails in the coffin of Gwinnett Place Mall as a viable business was the opening of Mall of Georgia in 1999. Mall of Georgia is an enclosed super-regional shopping mall located in Gwinnett County, Georgia.

Mall of Georgia basically took many of Gwinnett Place Mall's customers when it opened. The mall business can be pretty dog eat dog it seems. Sugarloaf Mills, the largest mall in Georgia, opened in 2001 and made Gwinnett Place Mall feel even less necessary.

(672)

Holly Wheeler is the sister of Mike and Nancy and Karen and Ted's youngest child. Holly is three years old at the start of Stranger Things. It is Holly who seems to sense there is a strange presence trying to communicate in the Byers house in season one.

(673)

E Pluribus Unum is Latin for "out of many, one." Sometimes it is translated more loosely as "one from many."

E Pluribus Unum was once the motto of the United States of America and references the fact that the cohesive single nation was formed as the result of the thirteen smaller colonies joining together.

(674)

The fact that Steve and Robin are wearing preposterous cosplay ice-cream store sailor suits in a real military base in season three is funny juxtaposition. Joe Keery said he was rather alarmed when he got the scripts and realised that Steve would be wearing this sailor costume for practically the ENTIRE season!

(675)

The ending of The Weirdo on Maple Street stresses the conflation of other dimension horror and gentle suburbia. The Upside Down can reach into the mundane trappings of our own world. It means that no one is safe - not even poor innocent Barb.

(676)

Eleven's head flick when she kills the orderlies and breaks Troy's arm in season one was an invention of Millie Bobby Brown.

Matthew Modine said he was rather alarmed at how much Millie enjoyed the scenes where Eleven has to kill or injure people!

(677)

Hawkins is a small Midwestern town located in (the fictional) Roane County in the state of Indiana. Prior to the events of 1983 it was a serene out of the way town where nothing much ever happened and the police had little to do. That certainly changed in the end!

(678)

The 'chapters' of Stranger Things are shrewdly engineered to end with cliffhangers and revelations so that you must quickly move onto the next episode.

(679)

Demogorgons featured in John Milton's Paradise Lost and Ludovico Ariosto's Orlando Furioso.

(680)

When she moves into the Wheeler basement, Eleven seems to be scared by the storm outside. This implies that when she lived in the Hawkins lab she never experienced thunder or lightning.

(681)

When Shannon Purser did her auditions for Stranger Things, the scene where Barb is being attacked by the Demogorgon at the pool was one of the scenes she had to perform.

They obviously needed to make sure they hired an actress who could be believably terrified onscreen.

(682)

The murky areas of the video game Metroid Prime 2 were judged an influence on the Upside Down in Stranger Things by some gamers.

(683)

Dacre Montgomery drew on his own experience on bullying when he took on the role of Billy Hargrove.

(684)

Benny's Burgers is small diner in Hawkins run by Benny Hammond. This is where Eleven goes to steal food when she first escapes from the lab. Benny's kindness in feeding Eleven and looking after her doesn't do him much good when he's shot by Hawkins Lab employee Connie Frazier. The logo for Benny's Burgers is inspired by the logo for Benny's Billiards in the Francis Ford Coppola film Rumble Fish.

(685)

In Stranger Things 2, Steve seems to be wearing the same red bandana to cover his face in the tunnels that Josh Brolin had in The Goonies.

(686)

The Duffers were so taken with Gaten Matarazzo that they allowed him freedom to fashion the character of Dustin in his own unique way.

(687)

Kali's powers are that she can trigger hallucinations in people and so project a fake reality. We see her make policemen see a fake blocked bridge tunnel in season two so she can escape with her gang after a car chase.

This car chase was shot in Atlanta but they couldn't find any long tunnels so had to use CGI. The Duffers said it was pure indulgence on their part to open season two with a car chase. They'd never done a car case before and couldn't resist putting one in the script.

(688)

Joyce having trouble with the two keys to the Russian drilling machine in the third season finale is a little homage to a scene in Superman III where Richard Pryor struggles with having to insert two keys into computers that are far apart.

(689)

Season one was designed to have an autumn atmosphere. This is why you see a lot of orange. Season two was more saturated and blue. Season three is probably best described as the neon season.

(690)

Joe Keery has over seventy lines as Steve Harrington in the season three episode The Bite. This is the most amount of dialogue that any cast member has in a season three episode. This fact is even more amazing when you remember that Joe Keery only became a full fledged cast member in season two.

(691)

The Phantom Zone prison dimension from the 1984 film Supergirl is sometimes cited as an influence on the Upside Down. You can see this film in Keith's video store at the end of Stranger Things 3.

Supergirl is a 1984 film directed by Jeannot Szwarc. The film was a spin-off from the Superman series and a vague attempt to launch a new money spinning franchise after Superman III had met with a mixed reception the previous year. Supergirl was written by David (The Dark Crystal) Odell and is rather incoherent and strange at the best of times, sadly lacking a consistent sense of fun and wonder. Although the film is never really exciting or inventive enough to ever justify its existence the casting department at least got a few things right. Helen Slater has just the right mixture of innocence and determination as Supergirl and looks great in her costume too - especially surrounded by flowers, bunny rabbits and hazy sunshine as she wallows in the natural beauty available on Earth.

(692)

There were a few articles after season two came out suggesting that the Flayer invading Hawkins was a commentary on imperialism (both past and present). While this was an interesting theory it seemed a bit of a stretch to think that Stranger Things 2 was designed around a subtext pertaining to colonialism.

It could be that these articles were thinking about War of the Worlds by H.G. Wells and applying it to Stranger Things. War of the Worlds is about a Martian invasion of England. At the start of the book the narrator of the story comments that the invading Martians are simply doing to Britain what the British Empire has done to various countries around the world.

(693)

The Mind Flayer is vaguely similar to a creature called Amygdala from the video game Bloodborne.

(694)

Sleepy Hollow Farm later turned Hopper's cabin into a Stranger Things themed escape room.

(695)

Some fans thought that Dustin secretly adopting Dart in season two was decidedly out of character because Dustin was the most logical and sensible of the boys in season one. Dustin appears blasé to the obvious dangers of adopting a creature from the Upside Down.

(696)

There was naturally a lot of (fun but inaccurate) fan and media speculation in the hiatus between seasons two and three. It was often reported that Kali would be back (which obviously didn't happen in the end) and there was even speculation that Max Mayfield would turn out to be a former subject at the lab like Eleven.

The source of this speculation seemed to be a combination of Max having special powers in a Stranger Things video game and the fact that she wore a lot of long sleeves (which would have hidden a tattoo) in Stranger Things 2.

(697)

The Duffers and Millie Bobby Brown tried to be a bit ambiguous about the fate of Eleven before Stranger Things 2 and pretend that they didn't know if she would be back or not.

This charade didn't really fool anyone because we all KNEW that Eleven would come back from the moment we saw Hopper leaving those Eggos in the woods at the end of season one.

(698)

The underground base that Steve and the Scoop Troop find themselves in during season three owes something to the Ken Adam sets in the old James Bond films with its gleaming metallic walls, retro futuristic vehicles, and long tunnels.

(699)

You can't help wondering sometimes who is supposed to be looking after Eleven in Stranger Things given that Hopper spends so much time away from home - although clearly this is one girl who can look after herself.

(700)

As Sadie Sink and Millie Bobby Brown were friends in real life, they lobbied the Duffers for Eleven and Max to be best friends in Stranger Things 3 so they could have plenty of scenes together.

(701)

Andrey Ivchenko was cast as Grigori in season three because of his uncanny resemblance to Arnold Schwarzenegger in The Terminator.

(702)

Brian Eddy designed a Stranger Things pinball table in 2019. It was the first table he had designed for twenty years.

(703)

Despite persistent gossip and speculation about her return, the Duffer Brothers said they never had any thoughts about bringing Barb Holland back to the show after her demise in season one.

(704)

Stranger Things fashion designer Kim Wilcox said the fashion of the individual boys at the Snow Ball dance is a clue to their future careers.

(705)

The hospital battle in Stranger Things 3 took two nights to film.

(706)

There was a rumpus in the media saying that Sadie Sink felt uncomfortable in the season two finale scene where Max and Lucas kiss but Sink put out a statement saying this was not true.

(707)

Netflix eventually dismantled the Starcourt Mall set - which felt like a shame. The reason behind this is presumed to be that they didn't want any intrepid fans to steal the props. The security on the site was also obviously costing them a lot of money.

(708)

The exterior shooting locations for the Wheeler, Sinclair, and Henderson homes in Stranger Things are all in the same locale. This is Piney Wood Drive, East Point, GA. This location was also used for Barb's house in season one.

(709)

Dustin's turtle in season two is named Yertle. Yertle is a character in the television show The Wubbulous World of Dr Seuss.

(710)

Visual effects expert Aaron Sims worked on Stranger Things and says the classroom showdown in the first season finale was an especially challenging sequence. What made this sequence difficult was that the Demogorgon had to be brightly lit (they had used it sparingly in previous episodes and kept it in the shadows) so the special effects had to be convincing. The computer effects were complex and as this was television (or streaming if you prefer) as opposed to a blockbuster movie, the special effects people were on a tight schedule. It is said that the special effects on season one were only completed days before the season was due to begin streaming.

(711)

This fight scene between Jonathan and Steve in season one seems to be a knowing wink to the extended battle in an alley

between Roddy Piper and David Keith in John Carpenter's
They Live.

(712)

Denis Villeneuve's 2013 movie Prisoners, a drama about a
child that goes missing, was a big factor in inspiring what
became Stranger Things. The Duffers watched Prisoners and
had the idea of doing a story like that as a television miniseries
and with a supernatural sort of twist. In this case the twist was
alternate dimensions and a monster.

(713)

Dustin's pet DemoDog Dart in season two trades on the Joe
Dante film Gremlins but also has something of Ridley Scott's
Alien in the manner that the creature sheds its skin and grows
very rapidly.

(714)

The beginning of season one has a reference right off the bat
when the scientist looks up in horror and is attacked in the lab
elevator by an unseen monster. This scene is designed to evoke
a similar scene in David Fincher's Alien 3 when the
Xenomorph strikes on Fiorina Fury 161.

(715)

The plot in Stranger Things 2 has deliberately keeps Eleven
apart from Mike and the boys so that she has her own 'quest'
(if you will). Looking back at Stranger Things 2 in retrospect,
this was quite a bold (if not universally loved) decision by the
Duffers. Their explanation was that they didn't want season
two to be exactly the same as season one and wanted to
surprise viewers with some of their choices.

This was certainly the case with Eleven in season two because
few people expected her to be confined to a cabin and then go

solo (even getting a solo episode that features only her) for much of the season.

(716)

There was gossip before Stranger Things 3 that Steve Harrington would now be one of Hopper's police deputies. While this was a nice idea, it had no basis in fact and simply seemed to be a fan suggestion rather than anything that was ever considered. Steve, circa season three, would still be a bit young for the police wouldn't he?

(717)

At the start of Stranger Things 2, Dustin fails to get the princess when he plays Dragon's Lair. This foreshadows the fact that he won't win the heart of Max.

(718)

In the original plan for Montauk, Jim Hopper was going to live in a shack on the beach and the Byers house was going to in the shadow of Camp Hero.

(719)

The makeup department were asked not to cover the kids in pancake makeup on Stranger Things 2 because the Duffers wanted a few spots and blemishes to make them look more like real kids.

(720)

The Georgia Mental Health Institute had an underground tunnel so that patients could be taken in (and out) without being seen by the public.

The Duffers said that some of the tunnel sequences they came up in season two were inspired by this tunnel.

(721)

The home of Joyce Byers in Stranger Things is a real house in Georgia that the set department found on the edge of some woodland.

The exteriors of this house were used while the interiors were shot on a soundstage in Atlanta. A number of fake walls were installed in the Byers set to be rigged with special effects. The Byers house obviously has to endure a lot of mayhem in the first season.

(722)

After Stranger Things 2 was released, Millie Bobby Brown's Instagram followers jumped from five million to 15 million.

(723)

Finn Wolfhard says he nearly gave up acting before he was cast in Stranger Things. Millie Bobby Brown has said the same thing.

(724)

Centipede, one of the games in the Palace Arcade in Stranger Things 2, was one of the first arcade coin-operated games to have a significant female player base.

(725)

Finn Wolfhard said that one thing he loves about Stranger Things is that there are obviously no scenes involving cell phones.

(726)

Francesca Beale, who portrays the lifeguard Heather in Stranger Things 3, originally auditioned to play Robin

Buckley.

(727)

Slant Magazine was one of the few places where season one of Stranger Things got a poor review. Their critic even slated the child actors and said that aside from Millie Bobby Brown they were all weak!

(728)

Eleven has the mask she wore while with Kali's gang in The Lost Sister hanging on her bedroom wall in Stranger Things 3.

(729)

The production of season one was a very low-key affair with hardly any media buzz. That would definitely not be the case when they shot season two. The first season was almost like a secret stealth project. There was no hype train. No one was following the day to day production too closely or combing for spoilers and set photographs. We had no idea who the Duffers were.

Stranger Things 2 was a different beast. Stranger Things 2 arrived with the burden of expectation. It was expected to be good.

(730)

The Demogorgon in Stranger Things seems to have regenerative healing abilities.

(731)

In his book The Montauk Project, Preston Nichols claimed (rather improbably) that the Montauk base known as Camp Hero was used for a mission to the pyramids of Mars using a 'vortex' that could be walked through!

(732)

Dacre Montgomery and his stunt doubles required 99 makeup department prosthetic wounds in total in Stranger Things 3.

(733)

Millie Bobby Brown said that when she had to go and pick up her driving permit she found that she was number (you guessed it) eleven on the waiting list.

(734)

Peggy Miley, who plays Mrs Driscoll in Stranger Things 3, had never heard of Stranger Things when she was cast. Peggy Miley said she met Millie Bobby Brown but not the other kids in the show because they were in school classes when she was shooting her scenes.

(735)

Shawn Levy feels that Stranger Things has a positive subtext in that the 'geeks' are the heroes and bullies are the villains.

(736)

Jake Busey says that some of the younger cast members in Stranger Things 3 knew who he was because they were fans of Paul Verhoeven's violent and satirical sci-fi film Starship Troopers.

Busey appeared in this fantastic cult film in 1997.

(737)

The plight of Will Byers in season two draws heavily on the plight of Regan MacNeil - the twelve year old girl possessed by the demon in The Exorcist.

(738)

The first Chevrolet van was released in 1961. The Hawkins Lab uses these vans in Stranger Things.

(739)

Chester, the Byers family dog in season one, was a tough cast member to work with according to David Harbour. They got rid of the dog because it wouldn't do as it was told on the set. One person who did love the dog was Millie Bobby Brown. Millie said that if she had to save one character in Stranger Things she would pick Chester.

(740)

There is a fan theory that the Upside Down is an alternate reality devastated by nuclear war. Some exponents of this theory suggest that Demogorgons are mutants who were once human. Maybe Demogorgons are what the survivors evolved into to survive in this hostile realm. How did Will survive in the Upside Down then in this toxic atmosphere?

One explanation for that would be that Hawkins, as an out of the way sort of place, didn't bear the full brunt of a nuclear strike. Maybe some of the radiation levels subsided by the time Will was trapped there.

(741)

Dustin has a Waupaca, Wis t-shirt in the first season Stranger Things episode The Flea and the Acrobat. This is the name of an iron foundry.

(742)

The Duffer Brothers said they sort of obsessed by Tim Burton's Batman film when they were kids and it made them watch other Tim Burton films when they came out. Tim Burton's second film Beetlejuice provided an early role for Winona Ryder so the Duffers were Winona Ryder fans from a young age. In fact, when they started shooting the first season of Stranger Things the Duffers said they were somewhat in awe of Winona at first because she was such a big icon to them.

Tim Burton's debut film, 1985's Pee-wee's Big Adventure, can be seen on a poster at the Starcourt Mall in Stranger Things 3.

Pee-wee's Big Adventure is a cult film that eschews unnecessary plot for the most part in favour of a series of comic vignettes and incidents that revolve around Pee-wee Herman (Paul Reubens) - a child-like man who always wears a small grey suit and red bow tie and lives in a Willy Wonkaesque house filled with colourful toys and gadgets.

(743)

The scenes in season three where Hopper takes Joyce to the abandoned Hawkins Lab to put her mind at rest were shot in a film noir way to add atmosphere.

(744)

The Stranger Things casting director Carmen Cuba said they were able to watch Finn Wolfhard's audition for Stephen King's IT before he was cast as Mike Wheeler.

(745)

The Duffer Brothers said that they have always had an endgame and ending in mind for Stranger Things. They want fans to rest assurred that they aren't just making this all up as they go along.

It always feels like a veiled dig at Lost when people say things like that doesn't it?

(746)

The 1983 John Carpenter film Christine - though set in the late 1970s - was an influence on the high school scenes in season one of Stranger Things. Christine is an adaptation of a Stephen King book.

In the plot, wimpy put upon teenage nerd Arnie Cunningham (Keith Gordon) purchases an old red-and-white 1958 Plymouth Fury car nicknamed "Christine" and lovingly begins to restore it. But ownership of the car seems to distort Arnie's personality over time. He becomes aloof and arrogant, the opposite of his former self. When a group of school bullies attempt to wreck Christine, the car seems to repair itself in ghostly fashion and - with Arnie behind the wheel - is soon out for revenge.

(747)

E.T. the Extra-Terrestrial is the most 'homaged' reference point in season one of Stranger Things. Some of these were intentional and others were not. It is clearly intentional that Holly Wheeler is dressed like Drew Barrymore was in E.T. the Extra-Terrestrial. It is very intentional that Eleven is given a yellow dress and blonde wig like E.T. It is also intentional that when Eleven and the boys are on bikes trying to escape from Brenner's team in Chevy vans, we think that Eleven will probably make the bikes levitate and 'fly' like they did in Spielberg's film.

(748)

Steve Harrington refers to Michael J Fox in Back to the Future as Alex P. Keaton quite frequently in Stranger Things 3. Alex P. Keaton was the name of Michael J Fox's character in the NBC sitcom Family Ties (which ran from 1982 to 1989). Family Ties was the second (after The Cosby Show) most watched show on American television in 1985 when Stranger Things 3 takes place.

(749)

The Demogorgon doesn't have any eyes. This is something it has in common with the Giger designed antagonist of Ridley Scott's Alien (although David Fincher's Alien 3 would later include some POV shots from the creature's perspective to suggest it had some sort of vision).

(750)

Max and Eleven are like a pair of little detectives in The Case of the Missing Lifeguard when they investigate Billy together.

This amusingly (and unwittingly) anticipates the fact that Millie Bobby Brown would later play Enola Holmes.

(751)

The Duffer Brothers said that before they made Stranger Things, they had asked Warners if they could make a new (this book was famously a 1990 miniseries with Tim Curry making a memorable Pennywise) television miniseries version of Stephen King's IT. It was the Duffer's favourite King book.

Needless to say, Warners rejected this approach and later made into a theatrical feature film. It is then something of a coincidence that Finn Wolfhard somehow ended up in both Stranger Things and IT.

(752)

Millie Bobby Brown auditioned for the part of Laura/X-23 in the Hugh Jackman film Logan but lost out to Dafne Keen. Millie said she did her audition in front of Hugh Jackman - which was a great experience even if she didn't get the part.

Had the part of X-23 gone to Millie it is very possible she might not have auditioned for Stranger Things.

(753)

The Duffer Brothers say they are quite dysfunctional apart and so always work as a team when they are writing and directing.

(754)

Paul Reiser said that his son is a huge fan of Stranger Things and kept badgering him for spoilers when he was cast as Dr Owens in season two.

(755)

Dr Owens quotes George Sarton in Will the Wise when he says - Men of science have made abundant mistakes of every kind. George Alfred Leon Sarton was a Belgian scientist and historian.

His most influential work was the Introduction to the History of Science, which consists of three volumes and 4,296 pages.

It is possible that Owens mentioning Sarton is a rather obscure joke. Sarton's wife was named Mabel. Mabel was also the name of Paul Reiser's daughter in the sitcom Mad About You.

(756)

David Harbour says he binged season one of Stranger Things along with everyone else when it came out.

Harbour said it was so engrossing he completely forgot that was him in the show.

(757)

The Duffer Brothers said they found it easy to write the child characters in Stranger Things because they largely based them on what they and their friends were like at that age.

(758)

Local kids who snuck into the derelict military base Camp Hero in Montauk said that some of the rooms had psychedelic wallpaper patterns. This strongly suggests that experiments with LSD took place there. While the Montauk conspiracies include an awful lt of outlandish stuff that is clearly not true it doesn't seem beyond the realms of impossibility at all that some MKUltra experiments took place there.

(759)

Universal Studios Hollywood created some Stranger Things themed treats to mark Halloween in 2019. These included Eleven's Waffle Sundae.

(760)

Hugh Everett III (1930–1982) was the first physicist who proposed the many-worlds interpretation (MWI) of quantum physics.

Everett's theories re used by Mr Clarke to explain the concept of dimensions to the boys in season one.

(761)

Brett Gelman, who plays Murray Bauman, said he played Dungeons & Dragons when he was a kid.

(762)

You can see Dustin's hat from previous seasons in Suzie's bedroom in the Stranger Things 3 finale.

(763)

Finn Wolfhard had some purple tints put in his hair to celebrate the end of shooting on Stranger Things 3.

(764)

Gaten Matarazzo's personal t-shirt design for his cleidocranial dysplasia charity had a Ghostbusters theme.

(765)

The Demogorgon figurine belonging to Mike Wheeler in season one only came out in 1984.

(766)

Many of the cast members in Stranger Things have said that when they were shooting season one they had a feeling that it could become like a little cult show with its own modest fanbase but they had no idea it would be such a mega successful mainstream show. The success of Stranger Things took them all by surprise. When they finished shooting season one the cast had no idea if there would even be a season two.

(767)

Will has a Panasonic RX-5090 Boombox stereo. Jonathan has a Fisher MC-4550. The television set in the Wheeler house that Mike so proudly shows Eleven is a 22-inch Mitsubishi. That TV set seems absolutely minuscule today! Joyce Byers has a Western Electric 554 Yellow Wall Phone. David Harbour said the kids in the cast were highly amused by 1980s telephones when they saw the Stranger Things sets for the first time.

(768)

The Duffers said that if they'd been casting Stranger Things a few years earlier they probably wouldn't have been able to hire Winona Ryder. However, by the time that season one of Stranger Things was casting it was increasingly common for actors associated with movies to do a (hopefully prestige) television show.

(769)

Jonathan and Nancy are known as Jancy to fans. Steve and Nancy were obviously known as Stancy when they were a couple.

(770)

Natalia Dyer was born in Nashville, Tennessee. Her first role was as Clarissa Granger in Hannah Montana: The Movie in 2009.

(771)

Despite the 'Satanic Panic' scare stories about Dungeons & Dragons, Gary Gygax, one of the co-creators of the game, was actually a regular church goer in real life. The newsclip at the end of Stranger Things 3 mentions the controversies related to Dungeons & Dragons.

(772)

The Stranger Things title theme was actually based on an old demo that Kyle Dixon and Michael Stein had lying around. When they were hired to compose the music for Stranger Things they thought the demo would be perfect for the title theme.

It needed a lot of work though. Their main task was to make the music feel bigger and bolder. It had to sound more cinematic.

(773)

It is estimated that, in all, fifty-eight characters people died in the first three seasons of Stranger Things. Many of these are unnamed background characters like scientists or Russian soldiers.

(774)

When he was asked who the best actor in Stranger Things was, Finn Wolfhard took the sensible diplomatic approach and said they were all great!

(775)

The full list of songs used in Stranger Things 3 are -

(SUZIE, DO YOU COPY?) The Red Army Is The Strongest by The Red Army Choir, Never Surrender by Corey Hart, Open The Door by Gentlemen Afterdark, Rock This Town by The Stray Cats, Movin' in Stereo by The Cars, Workin' For A Livin by Huey Lewis And The News, She's Got You by Patsy Cline, Hot Blooded by Foreigner, Can't Fight This Feeling by REO Speedwagon, (I Just) Died In Your Arms by Cutting Crew.

(THE MALL RATS) You Don't Mess Around With Jim by Jim Croce, Get Up and Go by The Go-Go's, My Bologna by Weird Al Yankovic, Material Girl by Madonna, Cold As Ice by Foreigner.

(THE CASE OF THE MISSING LIFEGUARD) Angel by Madonna, Lovergirl by Teena Marie, Things Can Only Get Better by Howard Jones, Wake Me Up (Before You Go Go) by Wham!, American Pie by Don McLean.

(THE SAUNA TEST) We'll Meet Again by Vera Lynn.

(E PLURIBUS UNUM) Stand up And Meet Your Brother by Possum River, Neutron Dance by The Poynter Sisters.

(THE BITE) R.O.C.K. in the USA by John Mellencamp.

(THE BATTLE OF STARCOURT) Higher and Higher by Jackie Wilson, Never Ending Story by Limahl, Heroes by Peter Gabriel.

(776)

Shannon Purser as Barb was given frumpier clothes than Nancy Wheeler to visually signpost her status as someone who is not a natural part of the cool teen cliques.

(777)

Hopper and Joyce are known as Jopper to fans who want them to get together as a couple.

(778)

When they trying to pitch Stranger Things (or Montauk as it was at the time), the Duffers said that one television network executive told them they should just make the show about Jim Hopper on his own investigating the paranormal. It's a good job they didn't take his advice.

(779)

The pool party at Steve's house in Stranger Things (where Barb was killed by the Demogorgon) is a beach party in the pilot script. The pilot script still had the show taking place in Montauk by the coast.

(780)

The scene in Stranger Things 2 where the possessed Will is tied down and questioned is inspired by the tense blood test scene from John Carpenter's The Thing.

(781)

David Harbour was born in New York City and went to Byram Hills High School in Armonk, New York. He graduated from Dartmouth College in Hanover, New Hampshire in 1997. Harbour got his professional start on Broadway in 1999 in the revival of The Rainmaker and made his television debut in

1999 in an episode of Law & Order.

(782)

The clown who gave Bob Newby nightmares as a child is obviously inspired by Stephen King's Pennywise.

(783)

Joe Keery was 24 years-old when he played Steve Harrington in season one.

(784)

Finn Wolfhard, Charlie Heaton, and Natalia Dyer got temporary pizza tattoos to celebrate the end of filming on Stranger Things 2.

(785)

Chief Jim Hopper drives a 1980 Chevrolet K5 Blazer. Barb Holland has a Volkswagen but this Cabrio is a 1988 model. Joyce Byers has a 1976 Ford Pinto - Joyce is not the sort of person who can afford a new car.

Jonathan also has an old car, an early 70s Ford LTD. Steve has a sleek BMW 733i.

(786)

It has never been credited as an inspiration, but Eleven's hairstyle and clothes in Stranger Things 2 are uncannily similar to Alyssa Milano as Jenny Matrix in Arnold Schwarzenegger's 1985 film Commando.

(787)

The car Eleven throws at the baddies in the Starcourt Mall in Stranger Things 3 is a 1985 Chrysler Lebaron Convertible.

(788)

A 2020 poll in LadBible ranked Stranger Things as the best Netflix show. It took 53% of the vote.

(789)

Jonathan Byers is described as having dark hair down to his shoulders in the pilot script.

(790)

O'Bannon is the name of the state trooper who is part of the conspiracy to stop Will's body being examined in season one. O'Bannon is a reference to Dan O'Bannon, who wrote Alien and directed 1985's Return of the Living Dead.

(791)

In season two, Bob talks about moving to Maine and suggests that Joyce go with him. Maine is the home of Stephen King and the place where he sets most of his stories.

(792)

The 1978 remake of Invasion of the Body Snatchers was an inspiration for the organic plant like look of the Demogorgon and Upside Down. This film is also referenced in season two when Will gives a piercing scream and shakes in season two when the scientists burn the tunnels. In the movie, those turned into 'duplicates' by the aliens emit a terrifying scream when pointing out a human.

(793)

Mike Wheeler has a poster for Jim Henson's eighties fantasy film The Dark Crystal on his wall. Other movie posters we see on walls in Stranger Things are The Evil Dead, The Thing, Jaws, and Endless Summer.

(794)

In the season two episode Dig Dug, Lucas decides to tell Max what really happened last year in Hawkins and spins out the whole fanciful yarn. Max feels like she is being made fun of. Max thinks that Lucas made it up and suggests his story lacks anything new - a meta commentary on the pop culture 'borrowing' of Stranger Things.

(795)

The introduction to Billy in Suzie, Do You Copy? as a lifeguard at the pool being oogled at by bored suburban housewives (who naturally sip New Coke) is an amusing riff on sequences in Caddyshack and Fast Times at Ridgmont High.

(796)

One nice aspect to season two is that we get some glimpses into the home life of Dustin and Lucas - a device that makes them feel a little more rounded.

(797)

Notice how we see Eleven in gunslinger pose in the background as Dustin shouts at the departing and vanquished Troy and James at the quarry in the season one episode The Monster.

(798)

Gaten Matarazzo said his favourite ever Stranger Things co-star was the cat who played Mews in season two.

(799)

Finn Wolfhard was born in Vancouver, British Columbia, Canada. He made his television debut as Zoran in The 100, followed by a role in the long running Supernatural.

(800)

Eleven's buzzcut in season one rather evokes Jean Seberg as Joan of Arc.

(801)

Millie Bobby Brown said that, given a choice, she would choose blueberry Eggos if she REALLY had to eat some waffles.

(802)

Inspirations for the look of Joyce Byers in Stranger Things were Meryl Streep in Silkwood and Cher in Mask.

(803)

Season one of Stranger Things is considerably in hock to E.T but, interestingly, it does not seem to mine any of the personal elements that formed the basis of Spielberg's story. Many of Steven Spielberg's early films are told through the eyes of a lonely or alienated child because he was drawing on his own experience of childhood.

Elliott has an absent father in E.T because Spielberg's own father left the family home and this personally affected Spielberg for many years. Stranger Things eschews the subtext of Spielberg's eighties films. It doesn't feel as if there is anything too personal from the Duffers' own lives in season one when it comes to family. They mimic the fun and emotional manipulation of Spielberg's films but the family angst doesn't seem to be something that interests them much at all.

However, the early plans for Stranger Things DID include a subplot where Lucas is troubled because his parents are going through an ill tempered divorce. This subplot was jettisoned in the end. It could be that the Duffers felt there wasn't room for it or it could simply be the case that they changed their mind and decided it was a trifle too heavy a storyline to incorporate into the show.

(804)

Joe Keery didn't use a stunt double in the sequence where Steve fights the Russian soldier (and finally wins a fight) in Stranger Things 3.

(805)

Finn Wolfhard was under the weather when they shot the Snow Ball scenes in Stranger Things 2 but he managed to get through them in the end.

(806)

The broken kneecap Millie Bobby Brown was recovering from at the start of production on Stranger Things 3 was sustained when she slipped by the side of a swimming pool. Millie had to have a double for the bike riding scenes because her knee was still giving her trouble.

(807)

Joe Keery said that he was rejected at nearly one hundred acting auditions before he won the part of Steve Harrington. He was waiting tables to make ends meet when he heard the news that he'd been cast in Stranger Things (or Montauk as it was probably called at the time).

(808)

In the scenes in Stranger Things where the characters are talking on walkie-talkies, the script dialogue coming through the walkie-talkies is spoken to the actor on the set so they can react in a fairly natural way.

(809)

Winona Ryder had to convincingly convey all of Joyce's emotion, even the tears, in Stranger Things because she is allergic to the chemical actors use to make them appear teary eyed.

(810)

Inspirations for the look of Billy Hargrove were Randall Flagg (a villain in Stephen King's book The Stand), Rob Lowe in the 80s Brat Pack drama St Elmo's Fire, and Jason Patric in 1987 vampire film The Lost Boys.

(811)

David Harbour tends to put on weight before a new season of Stranger Things because he likes Hopper to look pudgy and a bit slobby. Stranger Things 4 is the first season he hasn't done this because Hopper is trapped in a Russian prison so unlikely to have piled on too many pounds!

(812)

Matthew Modine is a veteran film actor, most famous for his leading role in Stanley Kubrick's 1987 film Full Metal Jacket. His other film roles include Birdy, Short Cuts, Married to the Mob, and Pacific Heights.

(813)

A Stranger Things Edition Polaroid Camera was released in 2019. It was priced at $99.

(814)

Max dresses as Michael Myers for Halloween in Stranger Things 2. A famed and classic horror, shot on a shoestring budget, Halloween was a notable financial success for John

Carpenter and spawned inferior homages, copycats and several sequels.

The film begins on Halloween night 1963. In the (fictional) town of Haddonfield, Illinois, six year old Michael Myers stabs his older sister to death in his Clown Halloween costume after he spies her fooling around with a boyfriend. Young Michael is confined to an asylum where psychiatrist Dr Loomis (Donald Pleasence) studies him and comes to the conclusion that there is nothing human left in Myers and he must never be released. However, one dark rain lashed night at the asylum fifteen years later, the now adult Michael escapes (while being unwisely transferred for a court appearance, the idiots!) from the clutches of the distraught Loomis and heads back to Haddonfield - where it just happens to be Halloween once again.

The town is relatively quiet, save for trick and treaters and babysitters. One such babysitter is Laurie (Jamie Lee Curtis) and Laurie is about to experience the worst night of her life when Michael finally returns home. Michael Myers wears a Captain Kirk Star Trek mask spray painted white and a boiler suit in the Halloween movies. Shaw Levy said it was unexpectedly difficult to gain permission to use the Michael Myers mask in Stranger Things 2. As for Sadie Sink, she doesn't watch horror movies and had never heard of Michael Myers!

(815)

What really happened to Hopper's daughter Sarah? In the first season finale we see in flashbacks that she is being treated in hospital for what seems to be cancer (for Sara has no hair). Hopper is seen distraught in a stairwell. But we never see Sarah actually die and the stairwell is (much) later revealed to be identical to the one in the Hawkins Laboratory.

In the second season finale, Hopper tells Eleven that his daughter Sarah "left us". Interesting choice of words. To further expand the mystery, Sarah is seen with a similar stuffed toy to the one that Will has in his 'Castle Byers' hiding place in the Upside Down. There are many theories on what happened to Sarah. The most obvious is that she had some contact with the Upside Down or was taken by the laboratory during her illness.

(816)

The scene in season one where Jonathan and Nancy find the injured deer in the woods is inspired by Until Dawn. Until Dawn is an interactive drama survival horror adventure video game developed by Supermassive Games and published by Sony Computer Entertainment. The game takes place in a remote part of Canada and has a group of teenagers spending a night in a cabin on Blackwood Mountain. One year previously, two girls mysteriously vanished in this area. The teenagers come under attack from a maniac and - in true horror movie fashion - now face a battle for survival.

There is a lot of DNA from Until Dawn in Stranger Things. The deer scene in The Flea and the Acrobat in particular is almost identical to one in Until Dawn where Mike and Jessica are in the woods and encounter a wounded deer. Just as they contemplate putting it out of its misery the deer is yanked away by a mysterious force.

(817)

The back sequence in The Flea and the Acrobat which shows us how Brenner would put Eleven in a sensory deprivation tank to remote view Russian people of interest is influenced by Jonathan Glazer's 2013 film Under the Skin.

In Glazer's film, Scarlett Johansson is an alien entity who seduces men and kills them in a black room of nothingness which has a liquid floor.

(818)

The Demogorgon in Dungeons & Dragons lives on the 88th layer of the Abyss, known as Gaping Maw.

(819)

Pyramid Head, a creature in Silent Hill with no face, was one of the inspirations for the look of the Demogorgon in season one.

(820)

A Poltergeist reference comes in season two when Eleven uses the static of the television to try and contact Mike. The television set was famously used as a supernatural connection in Poltergeist. It is often alleged that a curse plagued the cast of Poltergeist. What is the evidence?

Months after the release of the film 22-year-old Dominique Dunne, who played Dana (the family's older daughter), was strangled in her own driveway by her abusive ex-boyfriend and removed from life support five days later. The death of Poltergeist's young Heather O'Rourke is perhaps the most convincing case for a curse. O'Rourke (Carol Anne in the movie) died of cardiac arrest and septic shock caused by a misdiagnosed intestinal issue. O'Rourke died in February 1988 at 12 years old, several months before the release of Poltergeist III, the final chapter in the original series.

Other incidents include Julian Beck, who starred as Kane in Poltergeist II: The Other Side, dying of stomach cancer months before the film even came out in theaters and Will Sampson, the actor who performed the exorcism, dying of malnutrition and postoperative kidney failure at age 53. In 2009, Lou Perryman, who played Pugsley in the original film was murdered in his own home by an ex-convict with an axe.

These deaths seem more like random and awful tragedies than

anything. JoBeth Williams, Craig T. Nelson, and Oliver Robins, who played the other members of the Freeling family in Poltergeist, are all still very much alive and would appear to rebuff any claims about a supernatural jinx.

(821)

Nancy goes to a party at Tina's house in Stranger Things 2. Tina and Nancy are the best friends in Wes Craven's A Nightmare On Elm Street.

(822)

Mike Wheeler ranks fourth in Stranger Things when it comes to the total screen time given to characters in the three completed seasons.

(823)

The Duffer Brothers said that before the first season of Stranger Things came out, Netflix warned them not to expect a huge amount of promotion. They assured the Duffers that Stranger Things would be a success through word of mouth.

This all proved to be surprisingly accurate. Netflix were obviously very confident that people would like the show.

(824)

Joyce Byers' Ford Pinto in Stranger Things is the same car as the one belonging to the under siege family in the film adaptation of Stephen King's rabid dog thriller Cujo.

(825)

Robin charts Steve's romantic rejections on a dry erase board in season three. These boards were not really used in 1985 though.

(826)

Hopper and Joyce's expedition to the Upside Down in the season one finale owes much to the crew of the Nostromo investigating the bleak storm battered LV-426 in the original Alien film.

(827)

There's some nice stuff in Trick or Treat, Freak between Mike and Will. We didn't get to see much of their friendship in season one because Will was absent for most of it, trapped in the Upside Down as he was. In this episode we see the close bond between them.

(828)

Millie Bobby Brown's mother did not want Millie to shave her hair to play Eleven in Stranger Things. Millie's mother, though understandably upset at the thought of her daughter's long hair being cut off, was obviously wrong about this in the end as cutting her hair off and playing Eleven made Millie not only famous but also a millionaire.

And as Millie pointed out to her mother, hair does actually grow back!

(829)

In an article, Rolling Stone magazine rated Stranger Things the sixteenth greatest horror television show of all time. The top spot went to Twin Peaks.

(830)

There is a crazy fan theory that everything which has happened in Stranger Things is not real and just a game of Dungeons & Dragons that Mike and his friends are playing! They never actually left that basement! It would explain why the show is peppered with D&D references and why the boys use the game to explain events and science. There is one big flaw with this theory. It would mean that the last episode would have to reveal the boys in the basement and hit us with the bombshell that Stranger Things was just a figment of their imaginations as they got engrossed in the game.

As far as shaggy dog endings go, this would rival the end of St Elsewhere where everything was revealed to be a figment of Tommy Westphall's imagination as he stared at a snow globe!

(831)

According to The Hawkins Middle School Yearbook/Hawkins High School Yearbook, the Snow Ball dance in season two took place on the 21st of December 1984.

(832)

In the early pitch document for what was then called Montauk, the Duffer Brothers wrote - 'Over the course of the series, the 'tear' or 'rip' that separates their world from ours will begin to spread over Montauk like a supernatural cancer. This cancer will manifest itself in increasingly bizarre paranormal ways. Electrical fields will be disrupted. Strange fungi will to grow on structures and people. A heavy fog will drift in from the Atlantic. The temperature will plummet. Food will rot. Gravity will fluctuate. People will glimpse bizarre entities in their homes and businesses. There will be an escalating number of 'vanishings.' The entire town will become 'haunted' – and in grave danger. If people can disappear ... can an entire town?'

(833)

When they were teenagers, the Duffer Brothers turned down an offer to study film at Florida State University because the university didn't want them to work together. They instead studied film at Chapman University in Orange.

(834)

The company Imaginary Forces created the title sequence for Stranger Things. The Duffers rejected some of the first designs for looking too modern and generic.

(835)

Music from Predator can be heard when Hopper investigates the pumpkin field in Stranger Things 2.

(836)

The secret knock that Hopper and Eleven use at the cabin in Stranger Things 2 is Morse Code for "us."

(837)

There is a Stranger Things parody cookbook called Stranger Fillings

(838)

When she did her auditions for the part of Max, Sadie Sink had to read some scenes with Caleb McLaughlin and Gaten Matarazzo. They obviously needed to see if she had good chemistry with the other kids.

(839)

The blonde wig worn by Eleven in season one cost $8,000 - which seems rather on the expensive side. Millie Bobby Brown hated wearing this wig because it made her head itch on warm days.

(840)

When the third season was released early for press reviews, journalists had to agree not to discuss any potential spoilers.

They were given a list of seventeen plot points they were not permitted to mention in any review. This seemed to irritate some of the journalists. They felt these restrictions left them with very little they could actually write about in their reviews.

If you look at the early press reviews for Stranger Things 3 you do notice how vague some of them are. The writers were clearly struggling at times to construct a review in which they couldn't mention the plot!

(841)

The Peterbilt truck that features in the season two episode Dig Dug is a meta reference the episode's director Andrew Stanton. Stanton directed the Pixar film Cars.

(842)

It needed 1,200 pounds of epsom salt to make Eleven/Millie Bobby Brown float in the kiddie paddling pool for The Bathtub. They did this for real - as per the instructions by Mr Clarke.

It was no fun for Millie Bobby Brown though because all that salt gave her a headache.

(843)

Joe Keery and Dacre Montgomery honed their basketball skills for weeks so that their big basketball scene in Stranger Things 2 would be more realistic.

(844)

The most powerful weapon in Dungeons & Dragons is the Vorpal Sword. This sword will make short work of most enemies.

(845)

In the sequence in season one where the kids are being chased on their bikes by Brenner's team and Eleven makes the lab van somersault into the air to clear a path, this stunt was done using nitrogen cannons to launch the van up in the air. The first attempt at this stunt went wrong and destroyed one of the cameras.

The Duffers got permission to stage the stunt again and thankfully it went fine this time. Netflix insisted that the 'flying van' image should feature in the trailer because they wanted a spectacular piece of action like this to help sell the show in the promos.

(846)

Despite his youth, Finn Wolfhard says he was already familiar with eighties bands The Clash, Joy Division, and New Order before he appeared in Stranger Things.

(847)

When the second season of Stranger Things became available on Netflix, fifteen million viewers streamed the new season inside three days.

(848)

The Stranger Things 3 premiere had a fair theme so the cast were able to enjoy some funfair rides.

(849)

Sean Astin said that when Stranger Things 2 was released to stream he stayed up all night following all the reactions and comments on social media. Although he had previously been in pop culture juggernauts like The Goonies and the Lord of the Rings movies, Astin said that Stranger Things 2 was the first time he had been part of a cultural phenomenon in the instant social media age so it was fun to experience the excitement online as it all happened.

(850)

Barb Holland's glasses are a homage to Martha Plimpton in The Goonies.

(851)

In the last episode of season one of Stranger Things, the boys play Dungeons & Dragons and remark on how short the campaign was. This subtext is the fact that season one of Stranger Things only consisted of eight episodes.

(852)

Nancy uses a Sony Cassette Recorder in Dig Dug. In the eighties it was common for music albums to be released on cassette and Walkmans (a portable cassette player with earphones that allowed you to listen to music wherever you were) were popular. The first Walkman was released in 1979. Cassettes were of course easy to use and record on too.

(853)

The pitch document for Montauk suggested the names Sam Rockwell or Ewan McGregor for the part of Hopper. The Duffers maintain though that David Harbour was the only person they ACTUALLY wanted.

(854)

Gaten Matarazzo said that shooting the scenes with Steve and the kids in the tunnels for Stranger Things 2 was probably the most exhausting sequence he has been involved in so far. Gaten said that everyone was pretty shattered and ready for bed by the time that particular sequence was in the can.

(855)

Stranger Things 3 earns a place in the heart of all George Romero fans by using 'Sarah Breaks Down' from John Harrison's amazing Day of the Dead soundtrack during a heart to heart between Steve and Robin.

(856)

In Dungeons & Dragons, the Demogorgon is eighteen feet tall. His heads resemble deranged monkeys and he has the power to hypnotise enemies.

(857)

Spielberg's Jurassic Park is referenced more than once in Stranger Things 2. When the DemoDogs sneak up on Steve at the junkyard this is a reference to Bob Peck's game warden being surprised by the Velociraptor. When Bob puts the power back on in the lab, Hopper quotes Jeff Goldblum in Jurassic Park when he says "Son of a bitch did it."

When something unseen is moving through the trees near the funfair in Stranger Things 3, as Holly Wheeler (who is, as in season one, far more observant than the adults around her) watches on, this sequence is heavily inspired by the arrival of the T-Rex in the original Jurassic Park.

(858)

The Mind Flayer monster in season two is often said to be inspired by Louise Bourgeois' spider like sculpture Maman.

(859)

On December 21, 2017, the body of 19-year-old Silling Man was discovered in a vacant Subway restaurant in the Gwinnett Place Mall food court. It was later established that the young woman had been murdered. The mall was obviously still derelict and abandoned when this happened.

(860)

Eleven's hairstyle in season two was based on the cover of the 1981 book Ronja Rövardotter by Astrid Lindgren.

(861)

The Mind Flayer in season two was inspired by lightning and volcanoes - awe inspiring and unsettling reminders of how powerful the natural world can be.

(862)

The pitch brochure for Montauk (as it was) visually cited the following films as inspirations - E.T. the Extra-Terrestrial, Close Encounters of the Third Kind, Altered States, Poltergeist, Hellraiser, Stand By Me, Firestarter, A Nightmare On Elm Street, and Jaws.

(863)

Priah Ferguson had never watched Stranger Things before when she was cast as Erica Sinclair.

(864)

Linnea Berthelsen, the Danish actress who plays Kali '8', mostly appeared in short films before Stranger Things 2. In 2014 she moved to England and studied at the East 15 Acting School.

(865)

The Demogorgon is mentioned in Voltaire's 1756 short story Plato's Dream.

(866)

In 1976, TSR, the company behind Dungeons & Dragons, launched Dragon magazine for players of the game. In the third season of Stranger Things we see that Will Byers has some copies of Dragon magazine at Castle Byers.

(867)

The Duffers have openly expressed the fact that Akira was an influence on Stranger Things. Akira is a 1988 Japanese animated film based on a comic. Akira is set in a future Tokyo and features psychics, telepathy, telekinesis, and secret government labs.

(868)

Millie Bobby Brown said that one eccentric makeup tip she has learned on the set of Stranger Things is that shaving cream will remove even the most obstinate makeup smudges!

(869)

The Duffers have confessed that the manga and anime Elfen Lied was an influence on Stranger Things. Elfin Lied is about a girl with incredible powers who escapes from a laboratory.

(870)

Natalia Dyer said she enjoys the whimsical eighties fashions that the costume department give Nancy Wheeler.

(871)

One of the curious things about the music in Stranger Things is that John Carpenter disputes that the Stranger Things score sounds anything like his work - which is rather odd as he was such a big inspiration.

(872)

Gaten Matarazzo said he felt he wasn't commanding enough for the part of Mike Wheeler and was much more suited to playing the quirkier Dustin Henderson.

(873)

The watch worn by Max in season two is a Swatch Yellow Racer.

(874)

The Duffer Brothers said that the kids in the cast were nervous when they first started shooting season one but they quickly grew into their parts and the nerves completely disappeared as the child actors became more and more confident.

(875)

The car that Hopper steals at the gas station in Stranger Things 3 is a Cadillac Eldorado Biarritz.

(876)

The comics we Eleven and Max looking at in Stranger Things 3 are issues 326 of Wonder Woman and 185 of Green Lantern.

In issue 326 of Wonder Woman, Wonder Woman follows Keith Griggs and Lauren Haley to the Central American nation of Tropidor on an investigative mission, and again encounters Tezcatlipoca.

(877)

The Duffer Brothers said the main reason they completely changed the arc intended for Steve Harrington was that Joe Keery was just TOO likeable to be a villain.

(878)

In the Starcourt Mall infomercial teaser trailer for Stranger Things 3, the Tom Clancy novel The Hunt for Red October is briefly glimpsed. This book is about a Soviet submarine captain who wants to defect and anticipates that the Soviets will feature in Stranger Things 3.

(879)

It took months to get permission from the Michael Jackson estate to use his song Thriller for the Stranger Things 2 trailer. Fifty other songs were considered but they were desperate to get the use of Thriller and so persisted. It was worth the effort. What they REALLY wanted was the narration on the song by Vincent Price. This gave the Stranger Things 2 trailer the perfect Halloween atmosphere.

(880)

It is Gaten Matarazzo who has the most lines in Stranger Things 2. His character Dustin has an impressive 356 lines in Stranger Things 2.

(881)

Before the success of Stranger things, the Duffer Brothers made a horror film called Hidden which sat on the shelf for a while and completely bombed at the box-office (despite some modestly decent reviews). The Duffers were devastated by the failure of Hidden and thought their careers in Hollywood might be finished as a consequence.

The film revolves around a family of three - Ray (Alexander Skarsgård), Claire (Andrea Riseborough) and their daughter Zoe (Emily Alyn Lind) - who eke out a secret existence living in a murky nuclear bunker eating canned food. Some sort of cataclysmic event has occurred and made it unsafe to venture up to the surface. The surface is stalked by some unknown monsters which the family refer to as 'Breathers'. The premise is vaguely similar to a more recent horror film called A Quiet Place but what makes Hidden more unique is the fact you get a huge twist which pulls the rug out from the audience near the end and makes us view the family and their plight in an entirely different light. The Duffers were clearly fans of Rod Serling it seems.

Hidden is not what you would describe as a lost classic but it is a solid enough horror entry with a more thoughtful script than many of these types of films go into production with. The last act of the film and the ending takes the viewer to places they were probably not anticipating and this element of surprise makes it a strangely rewarding experience for those who stick with it through the (much more familiar) early segments of the story.

The character building and methodical approach early in the film might stretch the patience of some viewers but it does reap its rewards in the second act of the film. The two lead actors lift the material up a few notches too and always manage to keep the characters interesting. Hidden is not a bullseye but it is an interesting low-budget thriller with more than a few surprises up its sleeve.

(882)

The website best-of-netflix.com ranked Jim Hopper as the greatest character in Stranger Things. Steve Harrington was second and Joyce Byers earned third place.

(883)

One thing that did concern the Duffers about Stranger Things was the sheer (and ever escalating) volume of TV and streaming content. There is now far more content available than any one person could ever hope to watch. The Duffers did worry that Stranger Things might potentially get lost in the crowd.

(884)

Natalia Dyer has the second largest number of lines in season one after Finn Wolfhard. Nancy Wheeler 346 lines of dialogue in season one. The Wheeler characters would have significantly less lines in future seasons though.

(885)

The first season was budgeted at $6 million per episode and the second at $8 million per episode. Netflix were coy about the budget for season three but it seems a safe bet to assume it was the most expensive to date.

(886)

Though they were disappointed by the failure of their movie Hidden to find an audience, the film did have a silver lining for the Duffer Brothers because M. Night Shyamalan enjoyed Hidden and so hired the Duffers to join the writing staff of his mystery show Wayward Pines.

The Duffers said that when they were developing Stranger Things they supported themselves with the money they had earned on Wayward Pines. You could say then that were it not for Hidden and Wayward Pines then Stranger Things might not actually have happened!

(887)

The mall montage featuring Max and Eleven in Stranger Things 3 was supposed to include a food feast and the girls getting their ears pierced but these scenes were not included in the end.

(888)

Gaten Matarazzo says he loves the eighties clothes he has to wear in Stranger Things and says costume fittings are always fun. Gaten said the one Stranger Things outfit he didn't like so much though was at the start of season three when Dustin has just come back from camp. Gaten said that Dustin's summer camp outfit was a trifle too small and tight for his tastes.

(889)

The Eggo brand of waffles were invented in San Jose, California, by three brothers, Tony, Sam, and Frank Dorsa. In 1953, the Dorsa brothers introduced Eggo frozen waffles to supermarkets throughout the United States. Eggos were known as Froffles at the time.

(890)

The production of a new season of Stranger Things is an increasingly complex and lengthy operation. Even when the actors have filmed all their scenes and gone home it still takes months to complete the digital effects.

(891)

There was a fan theory during season one that Hopper was really Jonathan's father. This was a popular theory as Joyce and Hopper clearly have some sort of history. We see too that Hopper and Joyce's estranged husband Lonnie dislike each other and Jonathan obviously doesn't like Lonnie either. Could Joyce have cheated on Lonnie with Hopper? Could Hopper be Jonathan's real father? In season one there are several moments where Hopper displays affection for Jonathan.

Another theory is that Hopper's is Will's real father. The fuel from this theory comes from the fact that Lonnie doesn't seem to care that much when Will goes missing whereas - by contrast - he seems quite pleased to see Jonathan when Jonathan goes to his house to see if Will is there. If Lonnie knew Will was Hopper's biological child it might explain why he apparently has less regard for him.

(892)

Hopper's uniform and car owes something to Chief Brody in Jaws. Jaws was an adaptation of a thriller novel by Peter Benchley and wasn't really expected to be the huge success that it became. The shoot was incredibly troubled and went over schedule and over budget - mostly because the mechanical shark they were given kept conking out and frequently proved to be useless. Steven Spielberg took to calling the mechanical contraption "the giant turd" during the aquatic sequences and had his hands full trying to get any footage at all that looked good.

It was remarkable really that with all these problems and his tender age he managed to deliver one of the greatest films ever made.

(893)

Winona Ryder made her film debut in the cult 1986 teen drama/comedy Lucas with Corey Haim and Kerri Green. She quickly became a prolific and much in demand teen actress with roles in films like Tim Burton's Beetlejuice, the cult black comedy Heathers, and biopic Great Balls of Fire! In 1990 she acted in Tim Burton's cult classic Edward Scissorhands and was nominated for a golden globe for her role in Mermaids with Cher.

Winona's talents were such that she worked with some of the most revered directors in the film industry over the next few years - Dracula for Francis Ford Coppola, Night on Earth for Jim Jarmusch, and The Age of Innocence for Martin Scorsese. The films that followed included The Crucible, Reality Bites and How to Make an American Quilt. In 1997, Winona played the android Call alongside Sigourney Weaver in Alien: Resurrection. Winona was asked to be in Alien Resurrection when the producers heard she was a big fan of Alien and had always wanted to be in a sci-fi film. Winona suffered a panic attack shooting the underwater sequence in the film because of a childhood incident where she nearly drowned at the age of 12.

In 1999, Winona was the lead actress and executive producer on her dream project - an adaptation of 'Girl, Interrupted', Susanna Kaysen's 1993 memoir about the two years she spent in the late 1960s at the famous McLean Hospital (of Sylvia Plath fame) in a psychiatric ward for teenage girls after a short session with a psychiatrist she'd never seen before. Ryder had spent seven years trying to secure the rights and bring the book to the screen. The film met with a mixed reception but it did propel the still relatively unknown Angelina Jolie to fame.

(894)

In the first Stranger Things comic by Jody Hauser, there are some panels where Will spies Nancy in the Upside Down as a result of her and Jonathan going out in the woods and Nancy climbing through the tree portal. Will sees that the Demogorgon is about to pounce on Nancy but distracts it by throwing a rock - thus allowing Nancy time to escape back through the portal. This section of the comic does provide an answer for anyone wondering how Nancy was able to get back into our reality so easily with the Demogorgon lurking.

(896)

Gaten Matarazzo says his favourite Stranger Things fan theory is that Dustin's girlfriend Suzie is a Soviet spy!

(897)

Back to the Future was the biggest grossing film of 1985 - the year that Stranger Things 3 takes place. No wonder that season three riffs on Back to the Future considerably. A script for Back to the Future existed as far back as 1981 but it was rejected by several studios as its writers Robert Zemeckis & Bob Gale had not had a hit film (despite good critical notices for Used Cars).

Disney were particularly appalled at the premise of a character falling in love with her time travelling son and felt the script was distasteful. It was only when Romancing the Stone was a hit in 1984 that Zemeckis had the clout to make Back to the Future and he found a champion in executive producer Steven Spielberg. Spielberg loved the script but didn't like the the Oedipal theme, which he described as "gross". When he saw how Michael J Fox and Lea Thompson played those scenes in the film he admitted he had been wrong. Fox made Marty deeply uncomfortable and Thompson made Lorraine innocent. Together they made the scenes funny rather than distasteful.

Like many great films the inspired casting of Back to the Future was somewhat fortuitous. After considering C. Thomas Howell, Eric Stoltz (best known at the time for the drama film Mask with Cher) was originally cast as Marty McFly but left the production after six weeks of production when Zemeckis and producer Steven Spielberg looked at the footage they'd shot and decided Stoltz wasn't right for the part. Stoltz was too serious and wasn't providing the humour they needed. He was trying to give too dramatic a performance.

They returned to a young Canadian actor they had considered before Stoltz. Michael J Fox was already well known through the popular sitcom Family Ties but his contract to that show made it incredibly difficult to get hold of his services. In the end, a deal was worked out and Fox practically went without sleep during the production, shuttling back and forth between Back to the Future and Family Ties. With his more natural gift for comedy, Michael J Fox was almost perfect casting. Much funnier and less aloof than the urbane Stoltz. Back to the Future made him a star. Fox said he was more or less Marty in real life and it wasn't difficult for him to capture the essence of the character. By the way, Sid Sheinberg (then head of Universal) wanted to call the film Spaceman from Pluto - a reference to Marty pretending to be an alien in George's bedroom. Luckily he didn't get his way on this.

(898)

Dacre Montgomery wore his own Saint Christopher necklace while playing Billy in Stranger Things.

(899)

Randy Havens said that after Stranger Things was released he found that people asked him a lot of science questions - which of course he couldn't answer because he wasn't a science teacher in real life.

(900)

According to The Hawkins Middle School Yearbook/Hawkins High School Yearbook, the ambition of Jonathan Byers is to be a rock photographer.

(901)

Steve Harrington seems to take at least one pounding in each season. In season one he was beaten up by Jonathan, in season two he was beaten up by Billy, and in season three he is beaten up by the Russians.

(902)

Finn Wolfhard says he has to wear a lot or protective gear when he goes skateboarding because Netflix (who produce Stranger Things) would be furious if he got injured.

(903)

When they were still pitching Montauk (soon to become Stranger Things), the Duffers cut together a concept trailer composed of classic eighties film clips backed with a John Carpenter score. Although there were no scripts when the actors were cast, the actors were all shown the test trailer the Duffers had designed using iconic moments from 1980s fantasy movies. The actors therefore understood what the Duffers were trying to do and were excited about the potential of the concept.

(904)

The Duffer Brothers said that Mike Wheeler was more of a 'straight man' in the early concept for Stranger Things but Finn Wolfhard's casting made the character funnier.

(905)

Matty Cardarople, who plays the Cheeto guzzling Keith, is the tallest Stranger Things cast member at 6'4. He only just edges out Matthew Modine - who is 6'3.

(906)

Finn Wolfhard said that during production of season one of Stranger Things, after he had done his scenes he was allowed to go back on the set by the Duffers to watch other scenes being shot so he could pick up some tips about directing. Finn said that being an actor is the best film school you could hope for because you learn so much on the set.

(907)

The Duffers had intended to shoot the Stranger Things 2 Snow Ball scenes in one day (the child extras had only been hired for eight hours) but this proved impossible so they had to get everyone back the next day. Even then, it was still a struggle and they only just managed to shoot everything they needed before the second day was through.

The child extras, in order to preserve secrecy, were not initially told they had been hired for Stranger Things 2 so it was a lovely surprise for them when they found out. The extras at the Snow Ball dance for Stranger Things 2 were originally told they were appearing in a show called Wonder View in order to maintain secrecy.

(908)

Millie Bobby Brown is generally regarded to have been the highest paid child star in the world circa 2017.

(909)

Stranger Things 3 continues the tradition of characters who have names beginning with B perishing. Benny, Barb, Bob, and Billy have now all shuffled off this mortal (and in this case fictional) coil.

(910)

A poster of Edgar Allan Poe's The Raven can be seen in the background when Nancy asks after the missing Barb at school in Holly, Jolly. This is what you call visual foreshadowing. They do a similar thing in season two when Dustin is searching for Dart in the school and you can see the word EVIL in graffiti on the wall.

(911)

Mark Steger, who played the Demogorgon in season one, said he got his love of monsters from the movies of Ray Harryhausen. Ray Harryhausen's trademark stop-motion animations and models memorably graced films such as Jason and the Argonauts, The 7th Voyage of Sinbad, One Million Years B.C., Mighty Joe Young, Clash of the Titans, and Earth vs. the Flying Saucers.

In this age of CGI it is of course especially charming to wallow in the work of Harryhausen and remember a time when it was models, puppets and matte paintings that took us to far off fantasy worlds rather than buttons on computers.

(912)

Matthew Modine turned down the part of Dr Brenner when it was first offered to him because he felt the character wasn't very well fleshed out. It took a personal intervention by the Duffers to persuade him to take the part.

(913)

Millie Bobby Brown said that she lost her voice five times shooting Stranger Things 3.

A lot of her screams in season three were done during post-production ADR (additional dialogue replacement or dubbing) in the studio because she hadn't been able to scream all the time on demand when they were actually shooting the third season.

(914)

In an early plan for season three, the Flayer monster was going to stomp on cars in Hawkins like a T-Rex on the loose in a Jurassic Park movie. They decided not to go ahead with this idea in the ed because they thought that - even for Stranger Things - it was a bit over the top and silly.

(915)

Cara Buono, who plays Karen Wheeler, said she reached out to the producers for a part in Stranger Things because she heard about the script and loved the concept.

(916)

Perhaps the single most eccentric Montauk conspiracy story came when the wrestler Rob Van Dam claimed to have stumbled into the area on his way to an arena and ended up in a time tunnel!

(917)

In 2018, a filmmaker named Charlie Kessler launched a lawsuit against the Duffer Brothers and alleged that Stranger Things had ripped off his 2011 short film 'Montauk'. Kessler's claims completely fell apart though when the Duffers produced 2010 email evidence of their discussions and plans for what eventually became Stranger Things.

(918)

Natalia Dyer said that on the night Stranger Things first became available to stream she noticed looks of recognition from strangers on the streets of New York. She said it was incredibly surreal and wild to think that she was now famous. Her experience was rather ironic because David Harbour, who lives in New York, feared the show was going to bomb because of what he saw as a lack of promotion. Harbour said that he didn't encounter any promotion or posters for Stranger Things in New York when the first season was imminent.

(919)

Some of the images of Will in the Upside Down in Stranger Things 2 with the snow like ash and dust of this shadow dimension swirling around him seem heavily inspired by similar shots of swirling dusty snow around the boy in Night Gallery's Silent Snow, Secret Snow. Silent Snow, Secret Snow is a famous story by Conrad Aitken. In 1971 it was adapted as a segment in the anthology series Rod Serling's Night Gallery - having previously been a 1964 short film. Both were directed by Gene Kearney. The Night Gallery version is a haunting and fragile tale narrated perfectly by Orson Welles.

(920)

Caleb McLaughlin was born in Carmel, New York. He studied dance for a year at Happy Feet Dance School in Carmel, NY and then at The Harlem School of the Arts. From 2012 he featured in The Lion King at the Minskoff Theatre. He was happy to play Simba on Broadway and had no initial thoughts about becoming an actor but changed his mind when some television auditions came his way. Caleb made television appearances in Law & Order: Special Victims Unit, Forever, and Unforgettable.

(921)

The costume department on season two said that old photographs of Johnny Depp and Bruce Springsteen from the 80s were an influence on the look of Billy Hargrove's clothes.

(922)

When Hopper becomes drunk at the restaurant in Stranger Things 3 after Joyce fails to turn up for their date, the background music is the drinking song from Giuseppe Verdi's La Traviata.

(923)

Although it is an anachronism for the arcade machines in Stranger Things 2 to have LCD screens (as opposed to cathode ray tube monitors) it was probably unavoidable because cathode ray tube monitors are difficult to capture perfectly when shot on film.

(924)

Stranger Things - of course - features the VCR (videocassette recorder). The most famous example comes when Mr Clarke watches John Carpenter's The Thing at home (despite the fact that the film hadn't been released on VHS yet as a rental at the time). The VCR was a big part of the eighties although, strangely, this technology actually lasted through the nineties too. Many people today of a certain age will nostalgically remember renting VHS tapes and going to the video store and it probably won't even feel as if it was that long ago. The idea of watching films on huge bulky plastic tape cassettes that you push into a VCR might seem preposterously old fashioned to young people who have no memory of them but this was technology that had a surprisingly long shelf life. VCRs were introduced in the 1970s and were still in relatively large use at the turn of the century until DVDs phased them out.

(925)

Gaten Matarazzo says the handshake between Dustin and Steve when they are reunited at the start of Stranger Things 3 was something him and Joe Keery came up with.

(926)

The relationship between Mike Wheeler and Eleven in season one is influenced by Tomas Alfredson's 2008 Swedish film Let the Right One In. Let the Right One In is also set in the early eighties and concerns two eleven year-old children - a boy named Oskar and a girl named Eli - who form a close bond. Oskar is bullied at school and Eli is a vampire. As with Eleven, Eli has to stay hidden and doesn't really understand the normal mundane everyday world. Like the character of Eleven, Eli also has special powers.

The Rubik's cube is an important part of the bond between the characters in Let the Right One In and we also see Mike Wheeler play with a Rubik's cube in season one of Stranger Things. The connection between Stranger Things and Let the Right One In is confirmed when the boys pretend Eleven is their cousin from Sweden in order to smuggle her into school and use Mr Clarke's ham radio.

(927)

Gaten Matarazzo said he was rather disappointed that they didn't get to shoot any school scenes for Stranger Things 3. He said he loves the school set.

(928)

The adventures of Steve's gang in Stranger Things 3 obviously supply a more expanded sort of role for Erica. Was this move justified in the end? While not all fans of the show were completely convinced that Erica's larger role completely worked (it is understandable if some found that her brusque injections of sarcasm worked better in small doses - as in Stranger Things 2), we have to see Erica's role in this season through the prism of eighties sitcoms - which usually featured a smartass kid with an endless battery of one-liners and sarcasm. Erica is the eighties sitcom kid who somehow tags along for the adventure. She is like a more blunt version of Arnold Jackson from Diff'rent Strokes.

(929)

Stranger Things owes a lot to the Stephen King short story The Mist. The story is set in the small town of Bridgetown, Maine and finds artist David Drayton and his son Billy trapped in a supermarket when a strange white mist engulfs their town. Could it have something to do with the secret military project said to have been carried out nearby and who do those strange tentacles belong to?

You can find The Mist in King's 1985 collection Skeleton Crew. This compilation is well worth getting hold of because it includes many memorable stories like Survivor Type, The Raft, Word Processor of the Gods, and The Jaunt.

(930)

During the shooting of Bob's death scene, Kate Trefry, a writer on Stranger Things, was the stand in for the DemoDog (which would be digitally added in later) that jumps on Bob.

(931)

Winona Ryder and Matthew Modine were rare amongst the

Stranger Things cast in that they'd known each other for years. They met for the first time when they appeared in the music video for Roy Orbison's A Love So Beautiful in the late 1980s.

(932)

Near the start of Stranger Things 2 you see Steve and Nancy working on an essay and reading it through. A real essay was knocked up by the crew so that the two actors would find it easier to react and have something that looked real. The essay was so terrible that you can see Joe Keery and Natalia Dyer struggling not to laugh.

(933)

Dustin suggests that the Soviets might be meddling with Promethium in their underground lair. Promethium is the substance used to create Cyborg in DC Comics. In the DC universe, Promethium was first developed by Dayton Labs, a company owned by Steve Dayton. It was a metal named after the Titan Prometheus.

(934)

Bob Newby famously works for Radio Shack in season two and is something of an electronics whizz. In the late 1970s, Radio Shack introduced the TRS-80, one of the first mass-produced personal computers. The walkie-talkies the boys use in season one are from Radio Shack but could be construed as an anachronism because they are believed to derive from 1985. Season one, as Stranger Things will be well aware, takes place in 1983.

(935)

One of the inspirations for Eleven is Madison the Mermaid in the 1984 fantasy film Splash. Like Eleven, Madison struggles to understand the world and uses television to try and expand her vocabulary. It's a completely alien world to Madison who is entranced by everything she sees, eventually picking up bits of English by watching television (crying at an episode of Bonanza!) and copying exercise shows. Madison, like Eleven, is endearingly inquisitive and strange in this baffled state of affairs.

Splash was directed by Ron Howard and written by Lowell Ganz and Babaloo Mandel. The film stars, amongst others, Tom Hanks, Daryl Hannah, John Candy, and Eugene Levy and won an Oscar nomination for its screenplay. In the film, Hanks plays Allen Bauer, a workaholic who runs the family produce business in New York with his more carefree older brother Freddie (Candy). A flashback at the beginning of the film reveals that, as a small boy, Allen jumped into the sea from a boat during a family holiday in Cape Cod, despite not being able to swim, after spotting something in the water. Underwater, he briefly met a young girl who duly saved him from drowning before he was pulled to the surface by his family. The instant connection he felt in that moment - which he comes to believe was a hallucination of some sort - has blighted his relationships ever since but, years later, Allen returns to Cape Cod to clear his head after a girlfriend dumps him and suffers a boating accident. The unconscious Allen is again about to drown before help arrives in the shapely form of Daryl Hannah, wearing the same necklace as the girl he met all those years before.

The eccentric mystery woman eventually tracks him down to New York via a wallet he dropped where they begin a seemingly perfect relationship with only one slight complication - unknown to Allen, his new girlfriend is a real life mermaid.

A minor classic, Splash is a charming and often very funny film that is lifted up an extra notch by the likeable and entertaining cast, especially a young Tom Hanks in his always enjoyable eighties comedy mode and the much missed John Candy. Despite the slightly weird 'high' concept this is a delightfully good natured and pleasant film that hasn't, with the possible exception of some of Daryl Hannah's Dynasty style shoulder pad outfits and a few cheesy bits of music, dated appreciably and is still a lot of fun.

Another plus is the unobtrusive direction which wisely allows the actors to take centre stage. The flashback sequence at the beginning of the film is quite arresting (and poignant) and once into the present day, or 1984 at any rate, Hanks and Candy immediately make a winning onscreen pair and give the film a lot of energy.

(936)

Stranger things 3 is festooned with Die Hard references. The white vest that Murray wears in the finale is a joke reference to John McClane in Die Hard. The elevator antics of Steve and the Scoop Troop offer more Die Hard references. Grigori even quotes a line from Die Hard to hopper when he says that policemen have 'rules' which must be obeyed.

Die Hard (which came out in 1988) takes place on Christmas Eve in Los Angeles. John McClane is a New York policeman who has just flown into town to see his estranged wife Holly and their two children. Holly is at her company's Christmas party high in the Nakatomi Plaza - a glittering high-tech skyscraper. McClane eventually finds Holly at the party but - while he is freshening up in the bathroom - a group of highly sophisticated German terrorist thieves, led by super suave classic villain Hans Gruber, gatecrash the party and take complete control of the building and everyone hostage.

Their target is the $600 million in negotiable bearer bonds stashed in the apparently impenetrable vault of the Plaza and they will stop at nothing to get the money. As their elaborate plans are set in motion they gradually become aware that McClane, in a vest!, is loose in the skyscraper and doing everything he can to foil their brilliant scheme. A deadly game of cat and mouse begins.

(937)

When Dungeons & Dragons was first released as a board game they eventually had to make some changes because of complaints by the Tolkien estate. The Tolkien people were especially annoyed by the use of Hobbits in D&D.

(938)

One downbeat Stranger Things fan theory is that Eleven is still in the lab and the whole of Stranger Things was merely a fantasy or daydream she had. In the very unlikely event that this theory is true it would be an incredibly depressing twist for Stranger Things to surprise us with!

(939)

In season three, Mr Clarke is at home listening to My Bologna by Weird Al Yankovic when he is visited by Joyce. This song is a spoof of My Sharona by The Knack. My Sharona was used in the 1994 film Reality Bites, a film that had Winona Ryder and Ethan Hawke (Maya Hawke's father) as the leads. There is another Ethan Hawke Easter egg in Stranger Things 3 when we see a 'coming soon' poster at the Starcourt Mall for Joe Dante's 1985 film Explorers. A very young Ethan Hawke played one of the kids in this sci-fi fantasy film.

(940)

 The men at the Hawkins post mock Nancy in season three by calling her "Nancy Drew" when she tries to investigate the rat mystery. Nancy Drew is fictional teenage amateur detective in an extended series of mystery books written by Carolyn Keene (a collective pseudonym, used by Edward Stratemeyer and, among many others, by his daughter Harriet S. Adams). Nancy Drew's intelligence, courage, and independence made her a popular role model for many generations of young readers. The first Nancy Drew book was published in 1930.

(941)

The Duffers said that Voldemort from Harry Potter and Clive Barker were all key influences on the Mind Flayer. The intention was to create an unfathomable monster who couldn't be explained.

(942)

The young Maxine Mayfield in the flashback sequence in E Pluribus Unum was played by Sadie Sink's sister Jacey.

(943)

The Silent Hill video game series was a very obvious influence on the Upside Down. The town of Silent Hill is a fog bound haunted place where (unseasonable) snow and dust seems to cloud everything in murk and mystery.

(944)

The young cast members in Stranger Things often Facetime one another sometimes because they all live so far away. Gaten is in New Jersey, Finn usually in Canada, and Millie often in England.

(945)

Gaten Matarazzo said that before he got his breaks with The Blacklist and Stranger Things he would go to about three auditions a week and experience constant rejections. This is pretty standard for jobbing actors though. It can be a very tough business.

(946)

John Paul Reynolds, who plays Officer Callahan in Stranger Things, joked that he is the only cast member who is never recognised or asked for an autograph. He said his friends don't even know he's IN Stranger Things!

(947)

The watch worn by Alexei in season three is a Kirovskie Crab.

(948)

Gaten Matarazzo says the Stranger Things kids played a lot of Monopoly between filming on the first two seasons.

(949)

When you see Dustin and Steve in the Russian base waiting for the elevator to come down in Stranger Things 3 this was all CGI - even the elevator.

(950)

The films and music of film director John Carpenter were both a big influence on Stranger Things. John Carpenter is an auteur who writes, directs and also composes his own music. His principle hero is Howard Hawks (although Carpenter's work is more pessimistic) and many of his films are essentially modern westerns with horror, science fiction and action elements.

He was inspired to become a filmmaker by his love of Hitchcock, Forbidden Planet, King Kong and Ray Harryausen and his debut feature - 1974's Dark Star - started life as a $60,000 student project but so impressed during showings at film festivals it eventually gained a theatrical release.

The familiar trademarks and techniques of John Carpenter are empty rooms and streets (emptiness represents suspicion and generates anticipation), flawed Hawksian heroes we can sort of relate to, Pyrrhic victories, distrust of government and authority, electronic music with accentuating notes, a love of anamorphic Panavision, and minimal exposition when telling a story. Carpenter's most famous films include Halloween, The Thing, and The Fog. You can see the influence of these (and many more Carpenter films) in Stranger Things.

(951)

Finn Wolfhard said that making a new season of Stranger Things is sort of like going back to school. You meet up again with old friends and soon get back into the swing of things.

(952)

Millie Bobby Brown listened to the Beasts of No Nation soundtrack to get in the right frame of mind for the big reunion scene between Eleven and Mike in Stranger Things 2.

(953)

When the kids try and run away from Brenner and the agents in the school corridor in the Stranger Things season one finale, many felt this was a little easter egg pertaining to the teenagers in John Hughes' 1985 teen film The Breakfast Club trying to evade their teacher in the school.

(954)

When Finn Wolfhard did a quiz to see which Stranger Things character he was most like he ended up as Will Byers.

(955)

The rats in Stranger Things 3 were all computer generated. They did some test footage with model rats but decided they were not sufficiently realistic and convincing.

(956)

The Duffer Brothers said they had never watched the BBC America show Intruders when they cast Millie Bobby Brown in

Stranger Things. Millie drew high praise from no lesser figure than Stephen King for her work in Intruders. The Duffers cast Millie on the basis of her auditions rather than any previous work she had done. The main actors in Intruders were John Simm and Mira Sorvino. In the show, Millie played a little girl who is used by a serial killer to house his spirit.

Sadly though, Intruders only ran to eight episodes and did not perform well enough to earn a second season.

(957)

The explanation for the trouble in Hawkins in season three is that a part of the Flayer was left in our reality after the events of season two. The cloud that flew out into the woods after the Flayer was driven from Will in season two survived and searched for a new host. That host became Billy Hargrove but the Flayer needs more hosts. It intends to merge them together to create a new form - a big new monster.

(958)

Cliff Martinez, Trent Reznor and Atticus Ross were other influences on the music in Stranger Things by Michael Stein and Kyle Dixon. The Stranger Things theme is patently heavily inspired by Wanna Fight from the Only God Forgives soundtrack (by Cliff Martinez).

The Stranger Things theme also owes something to Abduction at Airport from the 1986 John Carpenter film Big Trouble in Little China.

(959)

Eagle eyed Stranger Things fans spotted an error in the Stranger Things 3 (One summer can change everything) poster. The poster shows Eleven bleeding from the right nostril but - usually - Eleven bleeds from the left nostril.

(960)

In the early eighties, computers in the home and office were
yet to become commonplace. Typewriters were still an
essential part of offices in 1983. In Stranger Things, Hopper
has a IBM Selectric III typewriter in his police office.

(961)

At the end of season two we hear a song by The Police called
Every Breath You Take is played. This song is actually about
an obsessed lover and stalking and has very dark undertones.
It is used to represent the mindset of the Mind Flayer after the
Gate has been closed. The Mind Flayer has been frustrated for
now but is still there, stalking the inhabitants of Hawkins and
biding its time.

(962)

The boys in the cast said they got fed up wearing shorts in
Stranger Things 3. They had to though because that season
was set in the summer.

(963)

There is a fan theory that Dr Brenner Has Special Powers. This
theory comes from the fact that Brenner - even in the midst of
Eleven's neck snapping antics - never seems to be afraid of
her. He's always calm and stoic, whether in the lab or hunting
Eleven down in the great outdoors (suburban Hawkins in this
case). Could it be that Brenner has powers himself which
explain why he is more intrigued by Eleven than afraid of her?

This theory suggests that Brenner is 001 when it comes to test
subjects and went on to run the program that created his
abilities. It's a fun theory but - at the time of writing - we
haven't seen any evidence for it being true at all in the show so
far.

(964)

Cary Elwes said that he came up with a backstory for Mayor Larry Kline to get a better understanding of the character. Elwes said he played Kline as a very insecure type of man who had issues with drugs. Elwes said that Kline's desire for power was a result of his insecurity and flaws. Kline is a composite of some real life politicians but Cary Elwes was tactful enough not to say which specific politicians. The name Larry is a nod to Mayor Larry Vaughn in Jaws. Larry Vaughn is the politician who wants to keep the beach open because he only cares about money and votes.

Appearing in Stranger Things 3 was nice for Cary Elwes because he enjoyed a screen reunion with Winona Ryder. Elwes previously worked with Winona Ryder on the 1992 Francis Ford Coppola film Bram Stoker's Dracula.

(965)

The Duffers say that Finn Wolfhard and Gaten Matterazzo were the most knowledgeable of the Stranger Things kids when it comes to eighties movies.

(966)

The Heathkitt ham radio belonging to Mr Clarke that the boys and Eleven use to try and contact Will Byers in season one appears to be a Heathkit DX-60. The term 'ham' means 'amateur' as in amateur radio.

(967)

When Stranger Things was released on Netflix in 2016 it quickly became one of the most talked about TV shows of the year. The children on the show were soon more famous and more in demand for television chat show appearances than most grown up actors. Those kids were seemingly everywhere.

(968)

The Lost Sister is by far the most poorly reviewed episode of
Stranger Things. What was it about The Lost Sister that
seemed to underwhelm many fans? Well, Kali's gang don't
register much as characters. The city backdrop and lack of
regular characters also obviously makes The Lost Sister feel
more like a generic piece of television than other Stranger
Things episodes. If you were dropped into this episode at a
random point and Millie Bobby Brown wasn't in the shot you
probably wouldn't even know you were watching Stranger
Things. After the high drama and action cliffhanger of The
Spy, it felt like a chore to some at times to sit through The Lost
Sister while we waited for the story in Hawkins to resume.

That was probably the biggest frustration fans had if one had
to speculate. It affected the pacing of the season and took us
away from the real danger and story. The structural intent of
The Lost Sister is to finish Eleven's journey of discovery so that
she knows more about herself and her powers before returning
to Hawkins to save the day. It's an interesting idea but possibly
one that didn't need an entire episode. Ultimately, The Lost
Sister just isn't very exciting - as least compared to the rest of
Stranger Things. It feels like an experimental sort of episode
that doesn't always quite work. It is debatable as to whether or
not this episode was completely necessary as the Duffers
insisted (they felt that Eleven's arc in season two was
incomplete without this story) and the end result was
something of a disappointment for many.

There were fans though who enjoyed the episode and didn't
see what all the fuss was about when it got a backlash. It would
fair to say though this was the most 'discussed' episode of any
season when it came to judging its merit.

(969)

The Duffer Brothers said they considered pulling The Lost
Sister episode from season two at one point but obviously

didn't do this in the end. Shawn Levy has described The Lost Sister as an interesting experiment that didn't quite work. The Duffers said they had fun making the episode and don't really regret it.

(970)

Hopper tells Eleven he'll be home at 5:15 in Stranger Things 2. 5 + 1 + 5 = 11.

(971)

Sadie Sink was judged to be too tall at her initial Stranger Things audition. They obviously changed their mind about this in the end.

(972)

Jake Busey said that he had no idea he was even reading for Stranger Things 3 when he did his audition. Those auditions clearly all become one big blur in the end. We can only presume the audition was rather vague to maintain secrecy.

(973)

The Duffer Brothers said that they suspected The Lost Sister episode in season might divide opinion. They turned out to be right.

(974)

Finn Wolfhard as Mike Wheeler has seventy lines in The Weirdo on Maple Street. This is the most lines any character has in any episode of season one of Stranger Things.

(975)

In the episode Dig Dug, Eleven hitches a ride from a trucker to 515 Larrabee. Think of what those numbers add up to.

(976)

Millie Bobby Brown's Twitter (which she has since deactivated) got a 105% boost in followers in 2017 after Stranger Things 2 came out.

(977)

Finn Wolfhard, who has been in a couple of signed bands, is honest and modest enough to have conceded that he most likely wouldn't have got a music record contract if he wasn't famous from Stranger Things.

(978)

When you see Will's body floating in the quarry in season one, that's actually a stuntwoman you see. They had planned to use a dummy but it looked far too fake so they got a stuntwoman to lie down and float in the water. She had to wear Noah Schnapp's wig and clothes to make her look like Will Byers.

(979)

The twins who alternated as Holly Wheeler in season one were no strangers to television and had previously played baby Judith on The Walking Dead.

(980)

Brett Gelman had a language coach for the scenes where Murray speaks Russian in Stranger Things 3. Native Russian speakers who are fans of Stranger Things think Gelman did a fine job in pronouncing the Russian words but probably would have been rumbled by the Red Army because his his accent.

Murray would probably not sound authentically Russian (or Soviet) to someone who really was from the Soviet Union - even if he was speaking in Russian.

(981)

Dig Dug is an arcade game developed and published by Namco in Japan in 1982, and later published outside Japan by Atari. The player controls Taizo Hori (originally known as Dig Dug in the time the game was released) to eliminate the underground-dwelling monsters Pooka and Fygar by inflating them until they pop or by dropping rocks on them. The style of this game was quite popular in the eighties. You might have played a similar game called Boulder Dash. The Duffers were not huge fans of Dig Dug but they couldn't resist using it as it anticipates Hopper trapped in the tunnels and even supplies an episode title in season two.

(982)

Bob Newby has a JVC GR-C1 camcorder in Stranger Things 2. This camera was an icon of the eighties and famously featured in Back to the Future.

(983)

The reason why the Duffer Brothers went off the idea of making Kali a thirtysomething man named Roman is that they simply couldn't find the right actor for the part. As a consequence of this they started auditioning women.

(984)

The lab room leading into the rift in Stranger Things 2 was heavily influenced by NASA's Space Environment Simulation Lab.

(985)

This sequence where Eleven takes out Brenner's agents in spectacular (if grisly) fashion in the season one finale is the most obvious example of the influence on Eleven of the character of Lucy from the manga Elfin Lied.

(986)

When he appeared in The Blacklist in 2015, Gaten Matarazzo played a character called Finn. This was quite spooky given that Finn Wolfhard would be one of his main co-stars in Stranger Things a year later.

(987)

Alec Utgoff's father is a renowned heart surgeon in Ukraine.

(988)

The password to enter Will's woodland Castle Byers is Radagast. Radagast is a wizard from Lord of the Rings.

(989)

The title of the season two finale seems like an obvious tip of the hat to the 1987 horror/fantasy film The Gate. The Gate was directed by Tibor Takács and is about two young boys who unwittingly release a horde of demons through some sort of portal hole in their garden. The film was a modest hit, opening at number two at the north American box-office, although the reviews were rather mixed.

(990)

The Stranger Things kids handed out peanut butter and jelly sandwiches to celebrities at the 2016 Emmy awards.

(991)

In 2020, there was another attempt to claim that the Duffers had stolen the idea for Stranger Things when Irish Rover Entertainment announced they were going to sue over their claim that the idea for Stranger Things was inspired by Totem - a screenplay by Jeffrey Kennedy (who is an actor and writer with minimal credits to his name). The lawsuit stated that

Totem was about a girl with supernatural powers who must help her friends find a portal gate to an alternative universe that is supernatural in origin. The lawsuit claimed that Stranger Things had stolen the plot, mood, setting (Indiana), and even the characters from Totem. Irish Rover Entertainment further claimed that Aaron Sims had worked on developing Totem and then took all of these ideas with him when he later worked on Stranger Things.

Netflix countered the new threat of legal action by saying that Jeffrey Kennedy had been peddling these conspiracy theories for years and that the Duffer Brothers had never heard of Mr Kennedy nor any screenplay called Totem. Netflix further accused Mr Kennedy of trying to secure money from Netflix for his 'baseless' claims.

It is of course fairly ludicrous to try and sue the Duffer Brothers for them having a similar idea to one of your own - especially when the similar idea in question is something that has been a constant staple of science fiction escapism for many decades. It would be like trying to sue the makers of Independence Day by saying that in 1976 you wrote a script about an alien invasion!

(992)

Finn Wolfhard said that the characters Mike and Eleven are a complete twist on the personalities of himself and Millie Bobby Brown because in real life she's chatty and energetic (like Mike Wheeler) whereas he is more quiet and reserved (like Eleven).

(993)

Any argument that season three is more superficial than what has come before can be countered by the emotional heft brought to the finale and the subplots where Hopper and Will Byers find themselves struggling with the inescapable nature of change and time passing.

(994)

Steve's BMW 733i E23 car in Stranger Things would (adjusted for inflation) cost around $80,000 in today's money.

(995)

Sadie Sink describes life on the set of Stranger Things as like being at summer camp.

(996)

In Prometheus Unbound, a four-act lyrical drama by Percy Bysshe Shelley, first published in 1820, the Demorgorgon is described as a "mighty darkness" rather than a demonic creature and it goes on to save the protagonist from years of torture.

(997)

Shannon Purser played Ethel Muggs in Riverdale after Stranger things. A '"Hashtag Justice For Ethel" moment in Riverdale was an in-joke, referencing 'Justice for Barb'.

(998)

Just before Stranger Things came along, a casting agent told Millie Bobby Brown that - at the ripe old age of eleven years - she was now too mature for most child roles and had missed the potential window to become a famous child actor. Happily, he was proved completely and hopelessly wrong about this.

(999)

The other cast members in Stranger Things 3 only heard the Dustin and Suzie Neverending Story song duet for the first time when the actual reactions of their character were shot. Their rather baffled and amazed reactions were therefore surprisingly genuine.

(1000) The Duffer Brothers say that when they are shooting Stranger Things they often dream about the show when they go to bed. There is no escape!

Lightning Source UK Ltd.
Milton Keynes UK
UKHW011839251122
412837UK00001B/60